DRIVE AROUND DENMARK

A handy guide for the motorist

ROBERT SPARK

TRAFTON PUBLISHING

Companion volumes:
DRIVE AROUND SWEDEN
DRIVE AROUND NORWAY

Photographs: Pages 33, 34 – Scandinavian Seaways; pages 35,
38, 40, 74, 76 (upper), 78, 79, 80 – Danish Tourist Board;
pages 36, 37, 39, 73, 75, 76 (lower), 77 – author.
Cover: Part of the picturesque Nyhavn in Copenhagen. Once
the haunt of sailors and full of bars it is now much more
respectable with numerous pavement cafés and restaurants
(photograph: Robert Spark).

Design: Peter Kerr Design Associates Ltd., 89A Quicks Road,
London SW19 1EX.
Maps: Stephen G. Spark.
Typesetting: Ian Greig Ltd., 132 Anyards Road, Cobham,
Surrey.
Printed in Great Britain by Butler & Tanner Ltd., Frome,
Somerset.

CONTENTS

	Page
An introduction to Denmark	6
Getting There	11
Driving in Denmark	15
Internal Ferries	22
Accommodation – Hotels, Inns, Self-catering, Camping	28
Food and Drink	44
Shopping	53
Attractions for Children and Adults	56
Sports and Recreations	70
The Itineraries	72
South Jutland, Funen and a Sprinkling of the Islands	81
Jutland Only	89
Mainly Central Jutland	99
Loitering with Intent	107
Accent on Zealand	114
For a Short Stay	123
Lightning Tour of Denmark	128
Copenhagen	132
Bornholm	135
The Smaller Islands	139
Helpful General Information	141
Index	143

BORNHOLM

SANDVIG ALLINGE
Gudhjem
HASLE SVANEKE
RØNNE AKIRKEBY NEKSØ
Dueodde

BALTIC SEA

Østerby Havn
LAESØ
Byrum

SWEDEN

ANHOLT
HALMSTAD

KATTEGAT

Rågeleje Gilleleje Hornbaek
Tisvildeleje HELSINGBORG
Sjaellands Odde Liseleje Helsinge Esrum HELSINGØR
FREDERIKSVAERK Hundested Fredensborg Humlebaek ILANDSKRONA
SEJERØ Rørvig Rungsted
Sejerby NYKØBING HILLERØD Vedbaek
Jaegerspris FREDERIKSSUND
Dragsholm Gerlev Org Farum
Gundstrup HOLBAEK Skibby
KALUNDBORG Shertinge Mørkøv COPENHAGEN
Jyderup MALMØ
Gerlev Ruds Roskilde Drager
Vedby Stenlille Viby Greve AMAGER
SORØ Strand
SLAGELSE RINGSTED KØGE
Glumsø
Halsskov Haslev Hårlev ST. HEDDINGE
KORSØR Rønnede
NAESTVED Fakse Rødvig
SKAELSKØR Mogenstrup Fakse Ladeplads
Menstrup Rude Tappenøje
PRAESTØ
Liselund
VORDINGBORG Kalvehave Møns Klint
Fejø Ferng Bogø STEGE
Tårs Torrig Kragenaes MØN
NAKSKOV Bandholm Alslev STUBBEKØBING
Søllested SAKSKØBING FALSTER
LOLLAND MARIBO NYKØBING
RØDBY Marielyst BALTIC SEA
Rødbyhavn NYSTED
Gedser

5

AN INTRODUCTION TO DENMARK

PROVIDING you are willing to accept its climate and topography, I can think of no better place for a motoring holiday than Denmark. Comparatively close to the UK (our nearest neighbour across the North Sea), it is easily reached by large modern ferries which eliminate the long tiresome drive which often has to be endured just to reach the country of your choice.

It is an easy motoring country, making it especially suitable for those with little or no experience of driving abroad. Food and accommodation are of a high standard, there are plenty of things to see and do, English is widely spoken and the Danes are friendly. So much for the commercial!

COMPACT AND VARIED

Denmark is the smallest of the Scandinavian countries with an area of 16,600 square miles (43,000 square kilometres) which makes it not much more than half the size of Scotland. It consists of the Jutland peninsula and 500 islands, of which about 100 are inhabited. The map in this introduction will show you how the parts of Denmark fit together.

There is a widely held belief that Denmark is flat and therefore scenically boring. This is a misconception. There may be no mountains (the highest point is less than 600 ft above sea level), no dramatic scenery, no wide surging rivers, but instead you have an ever-changing panorama: undulating countryside, lakes, small streams and placid rivers, forests and gentle fjords. There are many areas of considerable beauty while even the 'average' landscape is very easy on the eye.

With 4,500 miles of coastline you are never far from the sea and there is an abundance of good beaches with long stretches of sand (on the Jutland coast you can even drive from one town to another along the beach).

Around five million inhabitants provide a fairly high population density but this is not apparent, as four fifths of all Danes are town dwellers. In fact a quarter of the inhabitants live in greater Copenhagen. Away from the larger centres of population you will find quiet towns and villages and when you are exploring along the minor roads you have the feeling of being very much away from it all.

Agriculture is important to Denmark but, as in the UK, it has changed. There are fewer herds of cows grazing contentedly in the meadows, instead there are much bigger fields of cereal crops. Pigs, so closely associated with the great British breakfast, are rarely seen out of doors but are bred and reared under cover. Sheep, once a rare sight, are now more prevalent while the horse and pony population has risen by leaps and bounds.

Industry, on the other hand, has greatly expanded, but as this is a comparatively recent development, factories are modern and often located in estates on the outskirts of towns.

DESIGNED FOR TOURING

Denmark is a small and compact country which means that you can easily cover a lot of ground without an undue amount of driving. This encourages you to take it easy, rather than burn up the miles in order to get from A to B. It also means you have time to absorb what you see which adds to the enjoyment of your visit.

Although tourism is important, economically, to Denmark it has never been allowed to overwhelm any part of the country. Unlike many other countries there are no major resorts and no ranks of high-rise hotels (in fact Denmark is very much a low-rise country). There are, naturally, areas which attract a greater volume of holidaymakers but for the rest, visitors are just a welcome addition to the established local scene.

Roads are good, even the minor ones, while the islands add to your pleasure, whether you reach them by bridge or ferry.

PARTS OF DENMARK

The peninsula of Jutland (the Danes call it *Jylland*) stretches for 250 miles from the German border in the south to the northern

tip where the Skagerrak meets the Kattegat. On the west coast is Esbjerg, the port of entry for British visitors. The Jutland scenery varies from the flat marshlands of the south-west to the beautiful lake district in the centre of the peninsula and from large areas of heathland to extensive forests. On the eastern coast is the charming Djursland peninsula while the west coast offers mile after mile of firm sandy beaches, often backed by sandhills. There are two major cities: Århus and Ålborg, both with their own appeal and personality.

Funen (or *Fyn* to the Danes), linked to Jutland by two bridges, is often – and deservedly – called Denmark's garden isle. Picturesque thatched cottages and quiet moated manor houses and castles help to make this one of the most delightful parts of Denmark. The principal town is Odense, almost in the centre of the island, and the birthplace of Hans Christian Andersen.

Funen's main off-shore islands of Ærø, Tåsinge and Langeland are also most attractive: Ærø, an absolute gem, is reached by ferry, but the other two are connected by bridges.

Moving further east is Zealand (*Sjælland*) which is separated from Funen by the 18-mile wide Great Belt. Large ferries maintain a constant service across this busy stretch of water although work has now started on bridging it. Zealand also has its quota of beaches, forests, lakes and farmland but it is dominated on the eastern side by Copenhagen. 'Wonderful Copenhagen' is not just an empty phrase, it really is a most enjoyable city: friendly, with a compact centre, offering a wide range of attractions. Less than 30 miles away is Helsingør (often known to us as Elsinore) which is dominated by Kronborg Castle, famous as the setting for Shakespeare's 'Hamlet'.

To the south of Zealand are the islands of Lolland, Falster and Møn. You cannot get away from the fact that Lolland is flat, but it has some good beaches while Falster is similarly endowed but is a little more undulating. Møn, smallest island of the three, is different again having steep chalk cliffs on its eastern side. All three are linked by bridges, have some nice little towns and a lot of tranquil countryside.

Eighty-five miles away from the rest of Denmark is the Baltic island of Bornholm. This beautiful holiday island, with an area of 225 square miles has an attractive mix of rich farmland, white beaches, a rocky coastline and one of Denmark's largest forests. It is easily reached by ferry from Copenhagen and is well worth a visit.

A PLACE TO STAY

Denmark offers a wide range of accommodation: luxury hotels, inns, youth hostels, camping sites, summerhouses, farmhouses and apartments in town and country. Summerhouses are particularly popular, as are the holiday hotels. The latter are self-catering centres with apartments or flats and a central building providing a range of amenities.

FOOD AND DRINK

There is a separate chapter on this subject but to put it briefly: Danish food is appetising and enjoyable. There is considerable emphasis on fish and seafood (and very good it is) while typical Danish dishes feature quite widely as well as the usual 'international' fare. The famous help yourself 'Cold Table' (*Koldt Bord*) is not seen quite as much as it used to be, but I am pleased to report that the equally well known open sandwiches (*Smørrebrød*) are flourishing in all their numerous varieties.

Domestically produced alcoholic beverages mean beer – who doesn't know the famous names of Carlsberg and Tuborg – and aquavit (schnapps). Apart from one or two liqueurs, and something to keep the cold out or settle a hangover called Gammel Dansk, that is it. Wines and spirits are imported and while the former are fairly reasonable (and often bottled in Denmark) the latter are distinctly expensive.

CLEAN AND PEACEFUL

Denmark is a clean and neat country with high standards of hygiene, while the Danes tend to be an even-tempered and tolerant nation so there is little sign of the explosive situations which arise in some countries. This doesn't mean that the inhabitants never complain about their Government, income tax or some other imposition, but they are, in general, law abiding. They have a high standard of living and a very advanced social welfare system and are increasingly concerned about the environment. Denmark is the oldest constitutional monarchy in Europe, a parliamentary democracy and the only Scandinavian member of the European Economic Community.

WEATHER

Just as the topography of Denmark is ofter misunderstood by the British so is the Danish climate. It is a temperate climate with rather mild winters when compared with the rest of Scandinavia and variable summers (just like the U K). Summer temperatures average 18 - 25 deg C (64 - 77 deg F) but the weather is changeable and it changes quickly from sunshine to showers and back again. It is seldom completely calm and, in particular, the west side of Jutland has a reputation for being windy – which can be very exhilarating. Spring and autumn are often very enjoyable.

THINGS TO DO AND SEE

There is no shortage of things to do and see – ranging from fascinating remains of the Viking age to superb modern art galleries. There are many intriguing museums – particularly the open air ones – and plenty of opportunities for sports and pastimes: golf, fishing, swimming, sailing, riding, walking and cycling. At many places (and at an increasing number of hotels) you can hire a bicycle. There are well-surfaced cycle tracks and these are increasing all the time. Whereas in the past Danes cycled because it was their established mode of transport, now they do it more for recreation and the sake of their health. Incidentally, much of what is in this guide is just as valid for someone wanting a cycling holiday as for the motorist.

There are plenty of activities for children who are positively liked as opposed to being tolerated. After all, this is a country which has produced both Hans Christian Andersen *and* Lego.

DRIVE AROUND DENMARK

My aim in this compact guide is quite simple – to provide you with useful, practical information and, in particular, to take you to some of the most attractive areas of this small and enchanting country; to point you in the right direction and take you down some of the minor roads. You don't have to slavishly follow the itineraries – I encourage deviation! I hope you will share my enjoyment of this friendly country and that, like me, you will wish to keep returning to it. You will be warmly received by Denmark's biggest asset: the Danes themselves. Their friendliness and warmth more than make up for any lack of mountains, guaranteed sunshine or cheap wine. Have a good time!

The author would like to acknowledge the help received from the Danish Tourist Board, including the U K Director and his staff at the London office and the U K management of Scandinavian Seaways. Also to Danes all over their pleasant country for their ever ready desire to be of help.

GETTING THERE

Passenger ships have been sailing regularly between Britain and Denmark for over 100 years. The company that started this link across the North Sea – DFDS – is the same one that maintains the service today, although it now sails under the name of Scandinavian Seaways. I have been travelling on their ships for over 30 years and although there have been many changes during that time what has remained unaltered is my feeling that the best way to approach Denmark is by sea.

That could be regarded as a purely emotive point of view but there is a much more practical aspect to consider. Few people, in my experience, manage to get away on holiday without some last-minute pressures. When you travel by sea you know that once you have made it to the quayside and driven on board you can relax for about the next 19 hours. The same principle applies when you are on your way home: a comfortable crossing makes an enjoyable conclusion to your motoring tour of Denmark.

Scandinavian Seaways operate a year round service from Harwich and a summer only service from Newcastle, both to the west Jutland port of Esbjerg. In 1989 the Harwich service averaged four times a week between mid-March and the end of September. The Newcastle service in 1989 was twice a week from 8 June to 14 August. Both services are, however, subject to change each season.

THE SHIPS

The Harwich – Esbjerg route is maintained by three large vessels: *Dana Anglia, Tor Scandinavia* and *Tor Britannia* which are in the 14,000 / 15,000 ton range. This size of ship is a far cry from what is normally thought of as a car ferry and it puts them more in the small to medium cruise liner bracket. All three ships are modern, air-conditioned and stabilised and have bright, inviting interiors. Cabins are comfortable and well-equipped, each having its own shower and toilet, while the minimum-priced accommodation is in couchette cabins, which do not have their own individual washing facilities. There is cabin and couchette accommodation for all, so you don't have people dossing down in the lounges.

WHAT IS ON BOARD

The on-board amenities are extensive: lounges, bars, restaurant, cafeteria, shops, two cinemas, disco, sauna and children's play area.

The restaurant offers an à la carte menu which is changed at regular intervals, there is also a table d'hôte menu and 'chef's specials' plus the help yourself *'cold table'*. The latter represents good value (or very good value if you can really tuck away a lot of food). The cold table is a very appetising array of dishes: fish, sea-

11

food, cold meats, salad, cheeses and sweets plus several hot dishes. You help yourself and are encouraged to go back for more – as many times as you like. When my son was a teenager I always felt that the shipping company must have earned very little profit from him after his repeated forays to the cold table. Details on the correct way to tackle this Scandinavian culinary institution are given in the chapter on 'Food and Drink'.

In the morning the restaurant offers a help-yourself breakfast at a fixed price which improves in value the more you eat. You can have your traditional bacon and egg but this costs a little more. A nice feature is that all the bread and Danish pastries (yes, you have them for breakfast) are freshly baked on board.

The cafeteria has both hot dishes and such things as open sandwiches, pastries and fruit, plus a range of beverages. They often feature a dish of the day which is usually good value. Incidentally, service is included in the cost of meals and drinks in restaurants and bars and you don't need to add anything extra.

Live music for dancing is provided in the lounge in the evening while the disco is generally the haunt of the younger passengers on board. The cinemas (for which an entry charge is made) show first-run films with two performances an evening with a different film at each showing. In the morning there is usually a programme of cartoons for children.

Although the ships are all very much under the same management they are not run in a completely identical manner and there are small differences in what they offer on board. Food and beverage prices are standardised but the shops may differ in what they stock.

If you like to have a pre-dinner drink when you are on holiday it is advisable to buy your supplies on board ship rather than pay inflated prices for spirits in Denmark. On board, you can pay for what you eat, drink and buy in the shops in sterling or Danish kroner or use any of the best-known credit cards.

What is common to all three ships is the high standard of cleanliness and the well turned out appearance of the crew. The combination of size and quality of the ships and the efficient way they are run all help to make the sea crossing a very enjoyable part of your holiday. Of course the North Sea is not always placid, but the size of the ships and their effective stabilisers help to reduce the motion and if that is not enough, the information office on board has available some extremely effective pills. So don't be put off by tales about the North Sea.

The service from Newcastle, as mentioned elsewhere, is more prone to change in frequency. This also applies to the ships which are invariably smaller and older than those on the Harwich route. But they always have a full range of amenities on board, such as bars, lounge, restaurant, cafeteria and shops. They also offer a broadly similar range of cabin accommodation.

CABINS

Cabin accommodation on the Harwich – Esbjerg service consists of either single, two-, three- or four-berth cabins (with shower and toilet) or couchettes. There is also a more de luxe service called *Commodore Class*. With this you get a very spacious cabin in the best position with either a double bed or two single beds, shower and toilet, easy chairs, mini-bar, radio and room service. Your breakfast is included in the Commodore Class fare and you can have it served to you in bed if you want.

SAILING TIMES

The Harwich – Esbjerg service has convenient departure and arrival times. Departures from Harwich are normally in the afternoon or early evening with arrival at Esbjerg on the following day at lunchtime. The Esbjerg departure time is usually 17.30 (there are exceptions) with a next day arrival at Harwich at lunchtime. You have a good slice of the day in which to reach either port, while arrival times give you plenty of time for onward motoring, either to your first night stop in Denmark or your home, on your return journey. You have to check in at least 45 minutes before sailing (and Scandinavian Seaways captains are keen on punctuality and are not given to waiting for latecomers). The terminal is at Parkeston Quay and is well signed, while the road approach from the A12 has been much improved in recent years.

   The schedules of the Newcastle service are much more variable, altering each year, and therefore I feel it wiser not to give any departure and arrival times. Suffice to say that they are usually not quite so convenient as those from Harwich.

   The terminal for this service is not, in fact, in Newcastle but in North Shields. You take the A817 (Howdon Road) near the northern entrance to the Tyne Tunnel and look for the signed right-turn to Tyne Commission Quay.

   At Esbjerg the ships berth at Englandskajen and on leaving the port area the roads are clearly signed whichever direction you are going. If you are heading east on the E66 (the main road across Jutland from Esbjerg) you are routed around the town, avoiding the centre. Coming in to Esbjerg on the E66 the signs are equally clear.

   An alternative to the Esbjerg route is that opened by Fred. Olsen Lines between Harwich and Hirtshals in north-west Jutland. At the time of writing there is one service a week in each direction throughout the year except in peak summer (July – August). Crossing time is $25\frac{1}{2}/27\frac{1}{2}$ hours. The service is maintained by the *Braemar* which accommodates 1,456 passengers and 486 cars. Another possibility if you are going to south Jutland is the Scandinavian Seaways service from Harwich to

Hamburg – the drive to the Danish border doesn't take long.

You can also use one of the shorter sea crossings and drive through Belgium or Holland and Germany. You can then approach the Danish border at Padborg (south Jutland) or via the Puttgarden to Rødby Havn ferry, the latter port being on the island of Lolland. In either case you do have to put up with a long drive and I always feel you are entering Denmark by the back door.

The other alternative is to fly to Århus, Billund or Copenhagen and rent a car, but this, like the overland route, eliminates the sea crossing which, in my opinion, is a part of the holiday.

MONEY-SAVING PACKAGES

One way of cutting the cost of your motoring holiday without sacrificing your independence lies in the 'go as you please' arrangement offered by the inclusive tour side of Scandinavian Seaways. The basic package includes the sea crossing (passengers and car) together with five nights' accommodation with bed and breakfast at any one of a range of Danish hotels. There are 15 hotels to choose from. The duration of the basic package can be extended if required.

In 1989 the cost per person ranged from £226 to £266 depending on the number of people travelling together.

A basically similar arrangement is available which offers a choice of 20 Danish inns which are spread throughout the country, but perhaps a little thin on the ground in some areas. In 1989 such an arrangement with six nights with bed and breakfast at your choice of inns, cost from £217 to £257.

Scandinavian Seaways arrangements also cover other hotel holidays as well as those at self-catering centres, summerhouses, apartments, farmhouses and even camping sites.

REMINDERS

Finally some small points. On board the ships Danish time rules – OK! This can mean that as soon as you get on board you have lost an hour. Access to the car deck is not always permitted during the voyage so when you leave your car take what you need during the crossing but avoid having to heave heavy baggage to and fro (there are lifts, but a small overnight bag is much more satisfactory). Do not forget to lock your car (doors and boot) and switch off lights if they happen to be on.

If you leave the UK on a Friday or a Saturday remember that when you arrive in Denmark the banks (and shops) will be closed. Also the Danes have a number of public holidays that can catch you out – for example would you know when Great Prayer Day is celebrated?

DRIVING IN DENMARK

FOR THE BRITISH MOTORIST, Denmark must rate as one of the easiest European countries in which to drive. In fact, I would go further and say it is *the* easiest, because of its excellent road network, lack of natural hazards, modest amount of traffic and the generally acceptable level of competence and discipline of Danish road users. In addition the road signing tends to be good and towns are usually provided with adequate parking facilities.

All these features make it an ideal destination for the first time abroad motorist and should encourage those who may have qualms about venturing overseas with their car.

The disadvantages really reduce themselves to two: driving on the right and the Danish language. Driving on the right is common to all European countries, other than Britain and Ireland, and really presents no problems. Once you have been driving for a very short time it becomes quite natural. Care needs to be taken when starting off after a break or first thing in the morning or when you are on deserted roads. You also need to 'think right' at roundabouts and when turning. Overtaking also requires more care and a reliable front seat passenger can be a help - but the accent must be on reliable.

The language is not such a problem: the standard international road signs are used in Denmark and there are not that many domestic ones you need worry about (some of them are mentioned later in this chapter). As so many Danes speak English there is far less likelihood of difficulty if you have a problem with your car, or if you get lost or if you have an emergency of some kind.

One thing which you should have with you - particularly if you are going to make the best use of this book and get the most out of your holiday - are good maps. I cannot stress too highly the value of good maps as they do let you get so much more out of a visit to Denmark, apart from avoiding that 'I wonder where we are now' kind of feeling. I recommend the Færdselskort 1:200,000 which are published in four parts by the Danish Geodætisk Institut. Map 1 covers northern Jutland; Map 2 takes in central Jutland (from just a little north of Esbjerg) and the island of Samsø; Map 3 includes southern Jutland, Funen and the smaller islands of Tåsinge, Ærø and Langeland; and Map 4 covers Zealand and the islands of Lolland, Falster, Møn and Bornholm. You can get them at most major bookshops in Denmark and there are several map specialists that stock them in Britain, for example Stanfords Ltd., 12 Long Acre, London WC2 9LP. I always take them with me in the car and a useful feature is that the key to the various symbols and signs and so on is given in English as well as Danish. Another good Denmark map is the 1:300,000 scale example marketed by Roger Lascelles, 47 York Road, Brentford, Middlesex TW8 0QP, price £3.95.

The Danish Tourist Board's general travel information

folder on Denmark has a useful map which you can use for planning your visit but the scale is not large enough to explore off the beaten track.

THE ROAD SYSTEM

As I have already mentioned, Danish roads are good and present no problems. What is delightful to the visiting motorist is that many roads carry little traffic. Of course the trunk routes and some cross country roads are busy, particularly in summer. Also you have a considerable volume of commuter traffic, morning and evening, around major towns and cities. But on many roads motoring is still a pleasure.

Although the principal main roads have had numbers for many years, it is only recently that numbering has been extended to cover secondary roads. There are now three number classifications: E or European routes, primary roads and secondary roads. Where I have quoted road numbers in the itineraries later in this book they are, to the best of my knowledge, identified on the appropriate road signs.

Motorway construction started late in Denmark and even today the three major motorways are incomplete, with substantial segments still to be built. These motorways have the international 'E' numbers, being E3, E4 and E66. The E3 comes into Denmark at the south Jutland frontier with Germany and, keeping to the eastern side of the peninsula, extends to the north Jutland port of Frederikshavn. Here, there are ferry connections to Norway and Sweden. There are quite lengthy sections which are not yet up to motorway standard, although there have been some useful improvments in recent years.

The E4 starts at the ferry port of Helsingør (connection to Sweden), skirts Copenhagen and then moves south through Zealand, on to Falster, and across Lolland to the ferry port of Rødby Havn for the ferry link with West Germany. Here again it is not motorway all the way although the Storstrøm bridge, between Zealand and Falster, which was a bottleneck, is now avoided with the completion of an impressive new bridge to the east. The E64 is a short section from the port of Gedser (on Falster) which joins the E4 shortly before the new bridge is reached.

The remaining motorway is the E66 from Copenhagen, across Zealand, Funen and Jutland to Esbjerg. Again there are only certain segments completed but at least the Odense motorway bypass speeds up transit traffic across Funen.

If the motorway building programme has been sluggish then bridge building has been flourishing. Over the last 20 years numerous new bridges have been built, mostly to replace short ferry connections. There are now 26 major bridges spanning sounds, belts and fjords and all of them, like the roads and the

Limfjord tunnel at Ålborg, are toll-free.

What the Danes have achieved to a very great extent is the construction of bypasses around towns, and even villages. This has effectively removed heavy traffic from town centres, making life much more pleasant for the inhabitants. This means that you frequently have to leave the main road to get into a town. You need to watch out for direction signs; watch for those marked *Centrum*.

Larger towns pose a little more of a problem, but I cannot think of any which are really difficult. The worst examples are those where the local authority has had an inflated idea of its own importance and built an elaborate ring road which is not justified by what is in the middle.

Not only are bypasses popular but so are pedestrian streets. Here again, even quite modest towns have pedestrianised the main shopping streets. An alternative to creating a complete pedestrian precinct has been to allow traffic, but to provide a number of artificially created obstacles to slow it down. These cause traffic to reduce speed by having to zig-zag down the street, although sometimes these obstacles are regarded as merely something of a challenge to younger drivers. In general the pedestrian precincts have been dealt with in an imaginative manner and add much to the attractiveness of the town centres. Their introduction has often been linked to the restoration of buildings so that an appealing townscape has been created.

Before leaving the subject of roads it is worth mentioning that when the Danes decide to carry out major road-works it will often result in the complete closure of the thoroughfare. Traffic is diverted, sometimes over quite a distance, and in this case the sign to watch for is *Omkørsel* (diversion). Road-works are indicated by the word *Vejarbejde,* while road closed is *Vegen en spærret* and no through road is *Gennemkørsel forbudt.*

RULES AND REGULATIONS

In Denmark there are three basic speed limits: in built-up areas 50 km/h (31 mph), outside built-up areas 80 km/h (50 mph) and on motorways 100 km/h (62 mph). When towing a caravan or trailer the speed limit is 70 km/h (44 mph), Local signs may show lower or higher limits and the general rule is that you should adjust your speed to the prevailing circumstances.

There is no specific sign showing the permitted speed when you approach a built-up area (as with the '30' sign in the UK). Instead you take your cue from the town name sign which also includes a silhouette of buildings: that is where the 50 km/h limit begins. When you leave the town you will find the sign repeated, this time with a diagonal red line through it, ending the speed restriction. In the case of a speed limit offence you are liable to a heavy fine which has to be paid on the spot. If you cannot pay, your car may be detained – and the police do not accept credit cards.

As already mentioned, the basic rule is drive on the right and overtake on the left. You should give way to traffic from the right. In particular watch for the triangular red and white give way signs or the line of white triangles painted across the road (known locally as shark's teeth) which indicate that you must give way to traffic on the road you are entering. You must also give way to buses when they signal that they are pulling out from a bus stop and, of course, avoid travelling in a designated bus lane. Denmark has no trams so that is one less hazard to worry about.

What is particularly important is that at junctions or round-abouts you must give way to pedestrians crossing the road you are entering. When turning left you move across in front of the traffic coming from the opposite direction and turning left, not behind as in the UK. Major junctions often have painted 'turn marks' on the roads to guide you to your correct position. Traffic lights are similar to the UK but they are sometimes suspended from above the centre of the road. In some instances filter lights are incorporated.

Another important point when making a right turn is to watch for cyclists and mopeds. They usually have their own marked or separate track on the right hand side of the road and if they are going straight ahead you must give way to them. Where the bicycle/moped lane is only marked by a white line (and not a separate track) you should not cross it. In fact the golden rule is to keep a sharp eye open for cyclists – they have their rights as well as motorists.

Clear indications should be given when you are turning and, in particular, when you may be changing lanes on motor-ways or main roads. Copenhagen, like any capital city, requires more care and attention. On the whole, Danish drivers are con-siderate towards those with a foreign registration.

Your horn should only be used in case of danger, instead you can flash your headlamps as a warning. Dipped headlights must be used in the dark, in fog or under any adverse weather conditions and parking lights are not sufficient. Using only one headlight or spotlight is not allowed. Motorcyclists must use dipped headlamps, even by day and in clear weather.

The regulations say that cars with asymmetric headlights for left hand driving may only be used if the part of the lens from which the asymmetric beam issues is covered with some opaque material. The material – I always use black plastic insulating tape – is cut to cover the appropriate area and applied to the outer sur-face of the headlight. You can also buy kits for different makes of cars with the black self-adhesive material marked out to the right shape.

Perhaps one of the most important laws that affects visiting motorists to Denmark is that relating to drinking and driving. All the Scandinavian countries are tough on drink/drive offenders. You can be prosecuted for having either an excess of alcohol in the blood or for driving with an undue proportion of alcohol in the blood. And just to show the law is even handed on the subject you can even be prosecuted for the same offence if you are riding a horse. Prosecution for an excess of alcohol carries an almost certain sentence of detention or imprisonment. You are liable to prosecution if the quantity of alcohol in the blood exceeds 0.8 per cent. Moral: don't drink and drive.

If the front seats of your car are provided with seat belts then the law says they must be worn. A motor-cyclist must wear a crash helmet and this also applies, of course, to a pillion passenger. Carrying a warning triangle is another requirement.

When taking your car to Denmark you will need your valid driving licence (not a provisional one), the certificate of registration, and your car should have a G B plate or sticker. (If you are travelling with Scandinavian Seaways or taking one of their packages you will normally get a sticker with your tickets.)

An insurance 'green card' is no longer essential for a vehicle registered in Britain but having one is strongly recommended. Consult your insurance company on this point. It is also worth checking whether you are covered for damage in transit.

PARKING

An important aspect of motoring is parking. Fortunately in Denmark parking is not too great a problem. The Danes have quite sensibly realised that if a lot of people have cars they need somewhere to park them. For example, in towns where there are pedestrian streets there are invariably parking areas nearby and you just need to look for the 'P' signs as you near the town centre. Although there may be a limit on how long you can park, at least you will not have to pay (except in major cities).

These are the parking regulation signs you will see:

Parkering/Standsning Forbudt. No parking or stopping. Under three minutes stopping or stopping for passengers, or loading, is not regarded as parking.

Datostop/Datoparkering. Stopping or parking allowed on even dates on the side of the street with even numbered premises and on odd dates on the side with odd numbers.

Where limited waiting is permitted the times will be shown on the signs – hours shown in black are for Monday to Friday; in black and in brackets are for Saturday; and hours shown in red are for Sunday. Very often they only show Monday – Friday and Saturday times. Parking discs (*P-Skive*) are required whenever waiting is limited. You can get one, free of charge, from petrol stations, post offices, police stations, most tourist offices and some banks. When you park you set the hand on the disc to point

19

to the quarter hour following the time of arrival. The disc is then placed – facing outwards – against the inside of the windscreen on the side nearest the curb.

Parking is forbidden on or in front of pedestrian crossings, within 5 metres (16½ft) of a road junction, on cycle tracks, in front of fire hydrants, where the kerb near a bus stop is painted yellow or otherwise within 12 metres (39 ft) of a bus stop sign. You may park with two wheels on the pavement providing you don't inconvenience pedestrians and local police regulations allow it. (In Copenhagen parking on pavements is only allowed in marked areas.) Parking is not permitted in play streets.

In major cities with parking meters these are in operation from 9.00 a.m. to 5.00 p.m. or 6.00 p.m. Mondays to Fridays and 9.00 a.m. to 1.00 p.m. Saturdays. The maximum period is three hours and they accept one krone or 25 øre coins but some now also take five kroner or 10 kroner coins. In Copenhagen they have different charges, depending on the location of the meter.

If you park illegally you can get a written ticket placed on your car or you can be towed away which means you have to pay the tow charge, a garage fee and possibly a fine.

THE FUEL SUPPLY

Petrol stations are reasonably plentiful throughout the country and all the usual international brands are available. The vast majority are self-service (*selvbetjening* or *tank selv*). Many stations now have note acceptors which let you get petrol after hours. They take D kr 20 or D kr 100 notes and those I have seen have pictorial instructions which make them fairly easy to follow. Petrol is usually available in a choice of three octane ratings but small rural outlets may only offer one rating. Lead-free petrol is widely available and the pump is identified by the word *'Blyfri'*. One pump may well be for diesel so don't go putting the wrong fuel in your tank. Petrol is, of course, sold by the litre.

BREAKDOWNS AND ACCIDENTS

If you have a breakdown look in the telephone directory under *Automobil reparation* or call *Falck*. This is a national organisation which has fire engines, ambulances and salvage equipment. You can call Falck day or night and they will come out and if they can't solve the problem on the spot they will tow you to the nearest garage. They charge a fee for this service. Falck have over 100 centres all over the country.

There is also *Dansk Autohjaelp* (Danish Automobile Assistance) which has more than 60 service stations. Again you have to pay for the assistance provided. On motorways you can use the emergency telephones and you should specify whether you want *Falck* or *Dansk Autohjaelp*.

At major garages you are likely to find someone who

speaks English and all leading manufacturers have service work-shops in Denmark. Don't forget that value added tax at the rate of 22 per cent – labour and materials – is added to all repair bills.

Should you have the misfortune to be involved in an accident you should get in touch with the *Dansk Forening for International Motorkøretøjsforsikring*, Amaliegade 10, DK-1256 Copenhagen K – telephone (01) 13 75 55. Following an accident you should leave the car where it is and make sure all essential particulars are noted. It is suggested that if the vehicle is causing a serious obstruction you should mark its position before independent witnesses and if possible take a photograph of the scene. This seems to be asking a lot of someone just involved in an accident. If you want emergency services dial 000 (no coins needed in call boxes). Finally, don't forget to notify your own insurance company as quickly as possible.

The national motoring organistion in Denmark is the *FDM – Forenede Danske Motorejere*. They offer technical and legal assistance, together with general tourist information, to members of motoring organisations affiliated to the AIT. They don't have a breakdown service but they have offices in about 40 towns. Their head office address and telephone number is Blegdamsvej 124, DK-1200 Copenhagen Ø, telephone (01) 38 21 12.

PARKING IN COPENHAGEN

Parking meters (9.00 a.m. – 5.00 p.m. Mon – Fri, 9.00 a.m. – 1.00 p.m. Sat): D kr 3.– to 5.– per hour.

Kerbside parking, where permitted: one/two hours, parking disc required. Multi-storey car parks: usually open 6.00 a.m. or 8.00 a.m. to 8.00 p.m. or midnight. Some close on Saturday afternoons or Sundays. Average rates: 2 hours D kr 10.– – to 15.– rising to D kr 30.– to 40.– per day.

ROAD SIGNS – SOME EXAMPLES

No entry	*Inkørsel forbudt*
Diversion	*Omkørsel*
Cul-de-Sac	*Blind vej*
Road closed	*Vejen en spærret*
No through road	*Gennemkørsel forbudt*
One way street	*Ensrettet*
Exit	*Udkørsel*
Soft shoulders	*Rabatten er blød*
Road works	*Vejarbejde*
Danger	*Fare*
Right	*Højre*
Left	*Venstre*
Pedestrians	*Fodgængere*
Cycle track	*Cykelsti*

INTERNAL FERRIES

A QUICK glance at the map of Denmark is sufficient to tell you that ferries are an essential means of communication. Although many bridges have been built – and some are outstanding examples of the bridge builders' skill – there are still 46 internal ferry routes in Denmark, plus another 33 serving other countries. Car ferries are, in fact, a way of life, a basic requirement and, large or small, they operate with a humdrum efficiency which would put many other forms of transport to shame.

Crossing times vary from three minutes to eight hours and the sizes of the ferries range from workaday little vessels with space for a handful of cars to massive multi-deck examples which take over 400 cars at a time. Making a ferry crossing is a pleasant interlude in the day's driving and some routes provide a most enjoyable mini-cruise. Any route that takes around 20 minutes or more will have some sort of refreshment facilities on board, while the vessels on the longer journeys may have both a cafeteria and a restaurant, a kiosk, comfortable seating and even a children's play area.

The Danes make the most of their ferries – coming on board and sunning themselves on deck, consuming picnics, or having refreshments, reading, chatting or dozing. In other words, making the most of the break from driving.

On the longer routes you can reserve your car space and in summer this is certainly advisable. On several of the most important connections I would regard it as essential. On any of the services operated by the Danish State Railways (DSB) – with one exception which will be mentioned later – you can make the reservation at any railway station. On other routes the reservation can be made by telephone (your hotel or the local tourist office will oblige). In each case you need to know how long in advance you need to arrive at the ferry berth. On the internal routes it is usuallly quite minimal, such as 15 minutes before departure.

On the short crossings there are no reservation facilities and you just turn up and take the next available departure with space. Nearly all these operate a very frequent service although there are the exceptions which run 'on demand'. How long you may have to wait on some of these short non-reservable services is very difficult to estimate. It depends on the time of the year and the day of the week and, for example, if there are trucks or buses waiting to cross as these can rapidly fill up the deck space of a small vessel. You need to allow for some delays when calculating your journey time, particularly if it is in the peak summer period or at the weekend.

The cost of the ferry should also be taken into account and these of course vary greatly, depending on the length of the crossing. For a car and driver the single fare can range from D kr 20 (for a 10 minute crossing) to D kr 456 (for a seven hour crossing). Return fares sometimes offer a reduction and there are also some special offers: day returns, low season reductions and so on. On a few of the services to small islands, only return fares are available. There is no doubt that on one or two routes the small capacity of the ferries is one effective means of keeping the flow of visitors and their cars to reasonable proportions.

THE GREAT BELT MOTORWAY

By far the most important ferry route is that crossing the Great Belt (*Storebælt*) and linking Funen and Zealand. Imagine if you can what it would be like to have an 18-mile sea crossing half-way up the M1 and you have some idea of the importance of the Great Belt service. Vast car ferries are ceaselessly ploughing across the Belt from the purpose-built terminals at Knudshoved (Funen) and Halsskov (Zealand). However in a few years this will all change as construction has begun of a road and rail bridge from Funen to the island of Sprogø where there will be a road bridge and rail tunnel to Zealand.

Once on board the ferry and parked you can make for the restaurant, cafeteria, seating area or go on deck, but do check which staircase serves your part of the car deck and on which deck you are parked. The staircases have a letter (*Trappe A, B, C* and so on) and when it comes to seeking your car among 400 others on several levels you need to know where to find it.

The crossing time is an hour and as you approach your destination there will be a loudspeaker announcement. On the car deck there are two lines of lights above each line of cars. These are red until a lane is about to move when they change to green. Don't start up before you get the green otherwise you will be very unpopular with your fellow motorists. I should add that these lights are not always used. Reservations on this route are essential, particularly if you are heading for Esbjerg and the ship for England. If you miss your booked time you may have quite a wait and they will not make an exception for those with ships to catch elsewhere. If you arrive early you will often get on an earlier sailing, which means you can take it a little more leisurely on the next section of your journey. You can buy your ticket in advance or pay at the check-in booth. Tickets and reservations can be dealt with by Scandinavian Seaways in the UK as they are the general agents for the Danish State Railways.

There are several other important routes linking Jutland and Zealand and on any of these a reservation is desirable. They include the Mols Line service from Ebeltoft to Sj. Odde (duration 1 hour 40 minutes) which has very modern, large ferries; Grenå - Hundested (duration 2 hours 40 minutes); and Århus - Kalundborg (duration 3 hours). The longest service is that between Copenhagen and Rønne, on the island of Bornholm (duration 7 - 8 hours) and this has large well-equipped vessels with lounges, lying down and cabin accommodation.

OTHER ROUTES

Some of the services serving the smaller islands are highly enjoyable and of them I would rate the one between Svendborg and Ærøskøbing on the island of Ærø as the best. You sail down the Svendborg Sound, between Funen and Tåsinge, past some smaller islands to the idyllic little town of Ærøskøbing. It takes 75 minutes and on a fine day it is superb. Others play an essential role in any island-hopping itinerary (and there are several of those to be found in this book).

Earlier I mentioned there was one Danish State Railways route for which advance reservations are not available. This is the 20 minute link from Esbjerg to the island of Fanø. This is the island which you see as you arrive on your ship from Britain. Although there are frequent crossings (30 - 34 per day) the car capacity is very limited and in the height of summer this can result in a wait of up to four hours or longer before you drive on board. So if you have a little time to spare at Esbjerg and decide to take your car to Fanø bear in mind you might have a long wait to get back. There would be nothing more annoying than to be on the island and to watch your ship to England sailing away without you. So near and yet so far!

On the shorter crossings you frequently pay on board – the ticket seller somehow getting round everyone before the ferry arrives at its destination.

The approaches to the ferries, even the smallest ones, are always clearly signed and in the same way, on leaving the ferry your route is always well signposted.

INTERNATIONAL ROUTES

The 33 international ferry routes provide connections from Denmark to Britain, Norway, Sweden, Poland, East and West Germany and the Faroe Islands. Some of these are particularly popular with the Danes as they allow them to buy duty free goods – hence the reason that thousands of passengers cross stretches of water for no other real purpose than to enjoy themselves and possibly save a little money.

INTERNAL FERRY ROUTES

The figures in brackets are the number of departures per day (in summer). This is followed by the crossing time. The figure that follows is the cost, one way, for a car and two persons (1989 fares).

1. Copenhagen — Rønne
   (1 - 2), 7 - 8 hrs, Dkr 599

2. Ebeltoft — Sj. Odde
   (6 - 10), 1 hr 40 mins, Dkr 276

3. Grenå — Hundested
   (6), 2 hrs 40 mins, Dkr 297

4. Århus — Kalundborg
   (5), 3 hrs, Dkr 316

5. Halsskov — Knudshoved
   (21 - 29), 1 hr, Dkr 222

6. Korsør — Nyborg
   (18), 1 hr 15 mins, Dkr 165

7. Korsør — Lohals
   (6 - 8), 1 hr 30 mins, Dkr 220

8. Stigsnæs — Agersø
   (15), 15 mins, Dkr 81 (return)

9. Stigsnæs — Omø
   (9), 40 mins, Dkr 150 (return)

10. Kalundborg — Kolby Kås
    (3), 2 hrs, Dkr 213

11. Havnsø — Sejerø
    (6), 1 hr, Dkr 208 (return)

12. Holbæk — Orø
    (7 - 10), 30 mins, Dkr 46

13. Hammer Bakke — Orø
    (on request), 6 mins, Dkr 72 (return)

14. Kulhuse — Sølager
    (on request), 8 mins, Dkr 40

15. Hundested — Rørvig
    (22), 25 mins, Dkr 85

16. Tårs — Spodsbjerg
    (16 - 18), 45 mins, Dkr 187

17. Kragenæs — Fejø
    (20), 15 mins, Dkr 71 (return)

18. Kragenæs — Femø
    (7 - 8), 50 mins, Dkr 114 (return)

19. Bandholm — Askø
    (6), 30 mins, Dkr 114 (return)

20. Stubbekøbing — Bogø
    (18 - 20), 15 mins, Dkr 48

21. Bøjden — Fynshav
    (8), 50 mins, Dkr 127

22. Fåborg — Avernakø — Lyø
    (6), 30 - 60 mins, Dkr 70

23. Svendborg — Skarø — Drejø
    (4), 50 - 65 mins, Dkr 85

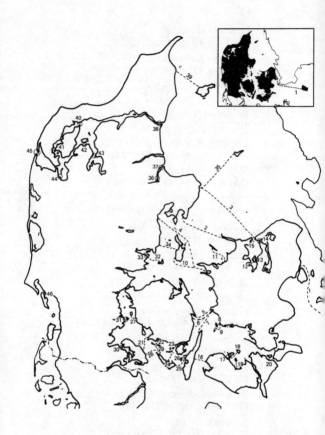

24. Svendborg — Ærøskøbing
    (5), 1 hr 15 mins, Dkr 131

25. Rudkøbing — Marstal
    (5 - 6), 1 hr, Dkr 140

26. Rudkøbing — Strynø
    (7), 35 mins, Dkr 80

27. Assens — Bågø
    (4 - 6), 35 mins, Dkr 51

28. Mommark — Søby
    (2 - 4), 1 hr 5 mins, Dkr 140

29. Fåborg — Søby
    (5), 1 hr, Dkr 140

30. Ballebro — Hardeshøj
    (29 - 33), 10 mins, Dkr 25

31. Årøsund — Årø
    (11 - 16), 7 mins, Dkr 40 (return)

32. Snaptun — Endelave
    (1 - 3), 1 hr 10 mins, Dkr 96

33. Snaptun — Hjarnø
    (20 - 24), 6 mins, Dkr 51 (return)

34. Hov — Sælvig
    (10 - 12), 1 hr 20 mins, Dkr 180

35. Grenå — Anholt
    (4, not daily), 2 hrs 30 mins, Dkr 510

36. Mellerup — Voer
    (on request), 5 mins, Dkr 27

37. Udbyhøj Nord — Udbyhøj Sud
    (on request), 5 mins, Dkr 28

38. Hals — Egense
    (80), 5 mins, Dkr 32

39. Frederikshavn — Læsø
    (4), 1 hr 30 mins, Dkr 250

40. Mors — Thy (Feggesund)
    (34), 5 mins, Dkr 24

41. Mors — Thy (Næssund)
    (34), 5 mins, Dkr 24

42. Branden — Fur
    (120), 5 mins, Dkr 38 (return)

43. Hvalpsund — Sundsøre
    (28 - 32), 10 mins, Dkr 38

44. Kleppen — Venø
    (55), 3 mins, Dkr 43 (return)

45. Thyborøn — Agger
    (15 - 19), 12 mins, Dkr 37

46. Esbjerg — Fanø
    (30 - 34), 20 mins, Dkr 121 (return)

(In some cases the car rate may vary and these fares should only
be regarded as guide prices.)

ACCOMMODATION – HOTELS, INNS, SELF-CATERING, CAMPING

THERE IS a wide variety of accommodation available in Denmark and the choice extends all the way from luxury hotels of the best international standard to camping sites. The motorist, being mobile, can of course select where to stay from the full range of accommodation, according to personal preference.

Apart from hotels in various price categories, there are inns (in Danish *kro*) many of which are very picturesque and old-established, and to be found in the country, in villages or small towns. There are the holiday hotels – self-catering establishments, invariably by the sea, which have become very popular in recent years while the highly successful farmhouse holidays are particularly suitable for families. Another Danish phenomenon is the summerhouse and these are to be found all over the country and provide another category of self-catering accommodation.

Youth hostels are available for those on a budget and they are open to motorists (of any age) while there are literally hundreds of camping sites to choose from if you want to keep expenditure to a minimum.

Nearly 1,000 establishments are listed in the Danish Tourist Board's brochure on hotels, pension, inns, motels and holiday centres. A copy is available, free of charge, from the DTB's London office and it is a very useful publication to have with you on your motoring holiday. There is no system of grading or stars for hotels, etc., so you have to be guided by price. Unfortunately a growing number of establishments do not include prices in the DTB's guide which is an annoying trend. Prices quoted (in the brochure or when you receive information direct from the hotel, etc.) will include service and VAT (known as *Moms*).

For accommodation in Copenhagen there is a central accommodation reservation office in the main railway station. You can call, telephone or write to make bookings and all categories of accommodation are dealt with including rooms in private houses. The address is Hotelbooking København, Hovedbanegården, DK-1570 Copenhagen V, telephone: (01) 12 28 80. Outside the capital the local tourist offices will assist you with the reservation of accommodation. A small fee will be charged for this service.

The principal hotels in cities, towns, in the country or at the seaside universally offer a high standard of accommodation. Bedrooms will invariably have a telephone and radio and often a TV, and sometimes a mini-bar, plus a well-equipped bathroom. Amenities will include a restaurant, bar and lift and, increasingly, a swimming pool, sauna and exercise room.

A number of new hotels have been built over the last two decades and these supplement the older-established premises usually to be found in the centre of towns. Not all of the latter have kept up with the times but although they may be more old-fashioned as regards decor and furnishing they are invariably comfortable and, of course, clean.

Also to be found throughout Denmark are mission hotels. These are all independently owned but have one basic characteristic – they do not serve alcoholic drinks. They offer simple, clean and comfortable accommodation, while their restaurants offer meals to match – plentiful and wholesome. Their prices are invariably lower than in other, licensed establishments, so they are well worth considering if you are travelling on a budget.

Perhaps the weak link in the range of Danish hotels comes when you are seeking what in Britain would be regarded as a two-star establishment. Some of those that fit this description are disappointing. Further down the scale are pensions which provide another grade of accommodation, while many tourist offices can arrange an inexpensive stay in a private house for you.

Guideline prices, for a double room (two persons) per night in the high season, for hotels, at the time of writing, are: Copenhagen – lowest category (room without bathroom) D kr 345–430; (room with bathroom) D kr 395–700; medium category (room with bathroom) D kr 675–840; highest category (room with bathroom) from D kr 750. Provincial hotels – lowest category (room without bathroom) D kr 175–280; (room with bathroom) D kr 215–400; medium category (room without bathroom) D kr 280–325; (room with bathroom) D kr 380–480; highest category (room without bathroom) D kr 325–600; (room with bathroom) from D kr 450. In most cases breakfast will be included in the prices.

Most hotels offer substantial reductions out of the peak summer season. Reductions are also usual for children when they have extra beds in the parents' bedroom, while some hotels have family rooms.

HOTEL GROUPS

There are several hotel groups in Denmark but at the time of writing they do not offer any particular advantage to the user, except possibly in simplifying the reservation procedure. They include *Dantop Hotels, Danway Hotels, Scandic* and *Best Western/Inter DK*.

INN CHEQUES

Cheques are available for accommodation at 65 Danish inns. Each cheque is D kr 195 and covers one overnight stay for one person in a double room with private bathroom and includes breakfast, service and VAT. At some inns a supplement of D kr 35 is charged and there is also a supplement of D kr 45 per night for a single room. There are reductions for children under 12. These cheques are administered by *Dansk Kroferie,* but details can be had from the DTB's London office.

Danish inns vary quite considerably and range from the old 'royal privilege' inns to modern ones which are much more in the nature of an hotel. They can be small with only a few bedrooms to quite large establishments. Often the original old building has been enlarged with a modern extension, sometimes with motel style accommodation.

Inns come in all shapes and sizes and can be found in towns and villages, in the country or by the sea or by the roadside. Some are as expensive as the better hotels and there are still plenty of the really picturesque kind: half-timbered, thatched roof and with an interior stuffed with enough bygones to stock a fair sized antique shop.

The food they offer is invariably good, wholesome fare, while quite a number have a deservedly high reputation for the quality of their cuisine. In the latter you will pay accordingly. You can always just have tea or coffee or a soft drink at a *kro* and they do not have bars as in a British pub – drinks being served at your table.

Some inns are well-suited to anglers, being close to rivers or with rivers actually running through their grounds. At others you will find such amenities as a swimming pool or children's play area.

Approximate prices for bed and breakfast for a double room are D kr 180–600. These rates will be a little higher for a room with a private bathroom – which is not always available.

SELF-CATERING

A development of the last 10 to 15 years has been the building of a number of self-catering holiday hotels. A typical example consists of blocks of well-equipped apartments, each having its own kitchen, bathroom, living room and bedrooms, and sleeping from two to nine persons. One building within the complex will have a range of amenities such as a restaurant or cafeteria, indoor or outdoor swimming pool, games room, sauna and solarium and children's play area. They are mostly by the sea, some being almost on the beach and, of course, they are ideally suited to family holidays. Also, as they may be relatively isolated, a car is essential.

Prices vary quite widely, depending on the centre and the time of year. In the summer the minimum stay will be a week but out of season you can stay for shorter periods.

No service is provided and you will do your own cleaning, make your own beds and so on, but the price normally covers final cleaning of the apartment. In some cases the cost includes electricity and water heating and you can hire bed linen and towels if you don't want to take your own.

Here is an example of the facilities offered in a typical

centre – the *Himmerland Golf and Country Club* near Løgstor on Jutland. Accommodation is in distinctive 'A' frame cottages accommodating two to six persons and having two bedrooms, lounge and dining areas, bathroom and kitchen. Equipment includes electric cooker, refrigerator, coffee machine and all utensils and colour TV. Facilities at the centre include 9-hole and 18-hole golf courses, indoor and outdoor pools, tennis courts, sauna, exercise room, table tennis, billiards, restaurant and bar. Activities range from riding to windsurfing.

Danland have six holiday hotels, which tend to be pretty big, three on Jutland, one on Fanø, one on Møn and one on Funen. They are built to different designs but the apartments are generally standardised and sleep either from two to six or two to eight persons. There are two or three bedroom arrangements, plus one which has split-level accommodation, and all are fully equipped. Facilities include indoor and outdoor pools, children's pools, sauna, billards, table tennis, TV lounge, restaurant and children's playground. All are close to the sea.

Typical cost for a complete apartment sleeping from two to eight persons for one week in the peak summer period is D kr 1,065–4,995.

Other holiday hotels – all broadly similar in concept – are at *Agger, Bønnerup Strand, Hirtshals, Blokhus, Søndervig, Lemvig, Øer, Bryrup, Skagen, Bork Havn* and *Henne Strand* (all on Jutland), on the islands of *Rømø, Møn* and *Fanø, Dageløkke* (on the island of Langeland), *Bogense, Fåborg* and *Svendborg* (Funen), and *Vedbæk* (Zealand).

FARMHOUSE HOLIDAYS

Over 20 years ago the Danes launched what has subsequently proved to be one of their most successful holiday ideas – the farmhouse holiday. The concept was a great successss and the farmhouse holiday continues to thrive and is one of the alternatives available to the visiting motorist.

There are two versions, one in which you stay on the farm as paying guests while on the other you cater for yourself in a separate apartment in the farmhouse or in a detached cottage nearby. All farms in the scheme are inspected by the local tourist association and one member of the farmer's family will be able to speak English.

When you are a paying guest you will usually take your meals with your Danish hosts and you will experience good, straightforward Danish cooking and be well fed. I have never yet heard anyone complain of anything except a certain amount of expansion around the waistline. You will be expected to keep your own bedroom(s) tidy, but that is the extent of your 'chores' although you are always welcome to help out if you want to.

When you are catering for yourself everything will be

provided except towels and bed linen and the apartment or cottage will include bedrooms, living room, kitchen and bathroom (with shower and toilet and hot and cold water).

Either version makes a good family holiday and they are very popular with children who regard the daily routine on the farm as extremely fascinating. In many cases the difficulty is trying to get them off the farm when their parents want to make an excursion to somewhere else. The other bonus of the farmhouse holiday is that many guests make an enduring friendship with their hosts. Some visitors have returned to the same farm year after year and quite a few farmers have made a return visit to the UK.

Farms offering accommodation will be found in most parts of Denmark and prices are standardised. At the time of writing the cost per person, per day is Dkr 200 (half board) or Dkr 230 (full board). There is a 50% reduction for children under 12 and a 75% reduction for children under four. The cost of the self-catering alternative is Dkr 1,100-1,500 for one week for an apartment sleeping four to six persons.

Although you will be in the country, you will never be very far from a town or the sea.

SUMMERHOUSES

Summerhouses are a Scandinavian speciality. In Denmark you will find them all over the country with considerable variation in their style, size and situation. They are mostly privately owned, the owner using his summerhouse for part of the year and letting it for the remainder. Various organisations handle the letting arrangements, often through the local tourist office.

The extremely wide range of designs and their furnishing means that the letting charges also vary considerably. A lot depends on location – near the sea or in the country, by a lake or near a town. Standard equipment and services will include electricity, hot and cold water, refrigerator, cooker (but usually with only heating rings and no oven), shower and toilet. Average size will be 540/650 sq ft and the interior will probably consist of a large open-plan living/dining room with the kitchenette at one end, bedrooms with bunk beds and the bathroom.

A summerhouse with two or three bedrooms, and sleeping four to six persons and having modern furniture and fittings would probably cost from Dkr 2,000 per week, according to location. A more luxurious, modern design, by the beach, and sleeping up to six persons and having a lounge/diner, modern kitchen, three bedrooms and perhaps a sauna would cost from Dkr 3,000 a week in the high season.

Prices out of season or in the shoulder months (May or September for example) are quite a lot lower. Some of these

Continued on page 41

The direct sea crossings to Denmark are operated by Scandinavian Seaways whose vessels provide a splendid introduction to Denmark from the moment you drive on board. Above, m.s. Dana Anglia and below, m.s. Tor Scandinavia, two of the ships on the Harwich – Esbjerg route.

ABOVE – Enjoying a meal on the North Sea in the restaurant on one of the Scandinavian Seaways ships. The range of on-board facilities make the crossing a pleasant and relaxing start to your holiday.
BELOW – The ship's restaurant introduces you to that Danish gastronomic speciality the Cold Table. Here you help yourself to whatever you want and as much as you want. A positive encouragement to gluttony!

A view over the rooftops of Ribe, Denmark's oldest market town, from the top of the cathedral tower. The town has a beautifully preserved medieval centre.

Denmark's most famous statue is the Little Mermaid in
Copenhagen. The story of the Little Mermaid was one of the many
written by a very famous Dane, Hans Christian Andersen. His
statue will be found on the corner of Copenhagen's Town Hall
Square. He appears to be looking in the direction of the nearby
Tivoli Gardens.

ABOVE – The most splendid Renaissance castle in Denmark is undoubtedly Egeskov on Funen. It is built on oak piles and surrounded by a moat and is in a 35-acre park. In the grounds is an interesting transport and horse carriage museum.

BELOW – Also on Funen and on the outskirts of Odense is the Funen Village, with a variety of typical old buildings – farms, smithy, mill, houses, cottages and so on.

*Denmark is well endowed with excellent sandy beaches. This one
is at Marielyst on the island of Falster.*

ABOVE – The Danish equivalent of the pub is the kro or inn. They vary enormously in style and appearance and no one example can be regarded as typical. Seen here is Munkebo Kro between Odense and Kerteminde on the island of Funen.

BELOW – Of great appeal to the family is Legoland at Billund in Jutland. It is now visited by nearly a million people a year and includes many different attractions as well as the huge mini-land made out of millions of Lego bricks.

ABOVE – One of Denmark's most striking and famous castles is Kronborg at Helsingør (also known in English as Elsinore). Overlooking the Sound that separates Denmark and Sweden, it was the setting for Shakespeare's Hamlet.

BELOW – Part of Brandts Klædefabrik, Odense's innovative and multi-purpose cultural centre.

dwellings are also suitable for winter occupation.

Prices do not include heating and lighting and you are responsible for the final cleaning or pay extra to have it done. You take your own bed linen, table cloths, tea towels and towels.

Another type of summerhouse is the *Kalmar* house. They are of typically modern Scandinavian design, built of wood and well-equipped. There are two versions, one sleeping four persons and the other five to six persons. They include a living room with wood-burning stove, electric heating, hot and cold water, kitchen alcove with electric cooker and refrigerator, bathroom, bedrooms and terrace with garden chairs. They are on sites on Jutland, Funen, Zealand and Langeland and have the advantage of being of standardised design. There are packages available from Scandinavian Seaways and a typical price per person (in summer 1989) was £161 for one week (based on four persons travelling together).

YOUTH HOSTELS

There are nearly 100 youth hostels located throughout Denmark and they can be used by people of all ages and whether you are on foot, bicycle, motor cycle or car. Many of the hostels have small family rooms, usually sleeping four persons as well as dormitory style accommodation.

Beds are provided with mattresses, duvets and pillows, but you bring your own bed linen (sheet, duvet cover and pillowslip) or a sheet sleeping bag of approved model and size (other types are not allowed). You can also hire bed linen at most hostels.

The majority of hostels serve meals which are very reasonably priced and packed lunches for the following day can also be ordered at many of them. Guest kitchens are available if you want to do your own cooking. You bring your own plates and cutlery but kitchen utensils are provided.

An overnight stay costs, on average, (1989) D kr 46 - 54 while there is a supplement payable when families use one of the family rooms. Advance booking is recommended for families and is also essential during the period 1 September - 15 May. There are certain conditions relating to the time of arrival, etc. For overnight stays a valid membership card issued by the Youth Hostels Association in the UK is required but failing this an international youth hostel card, valid for a year, can be obtained in Denmark (cost approximately D kr 98). Guest cards, valid for one night, are also available at a cost of D kr 18.

An official guide to Danish youth hostels providing full information on their location, the times when they are open and the facilities and meals that are available is obtainable from the Youth Hostels Association, 14 Southampton Street, London WC2E 7HY. In Denmark you can usually get a copy at tourist offices or at some booksellers or from *Danmarks Vandrerhjem,*

Vesterbrogade 39, DK-1620 Copenhagen V, price approximately D kr 35 plus postage.

The hostel buildings range from former manor houses to small cottages or modern purpose-built units. Interiors tend to be up-to-date while some of them have a swimming pool. An increasing number have special rooms and toilets for disabled persons.

CAMPING

Denmark probably has more camping sites for its area than anywhere else. There are nearly 500 approved sites to choose from and many of them occupy extremely scenic and well-landscaped settings. Apart from accommodating visitors with tents or caravans, some sites also have overnight cabins.

The Danish Camping Council inspects all sites at regular intervals and without prior warning, and they are placed in one of three categories: one-star, two-star or three-star. Minimum requirements are acceptable sanitary installations, drinking water and suitable ground. A two-star site must have showers, razor points, laundry and ironing facilities and a provision store not more than 1 km away. Three-star sites have to meet even higher standards. Many sites are well arranged with different areas screened by trees or hedges. They often occupy positions of considerable natural beauty. The better sites include a small supermarket and quite a few now have swimming pools and children's play areas.

A detailed guide to approved sites is published each year by the Danish Camping Council and can be obtained from *Campingrådet,* Olof Palmesgade 10, DK-2100 Copenhagen Ø, price D kr 65. The Danish Tourist Board also publishes each year a free brochure listing two-and three-star sites and also youth hostels. You can obtain a copy from the DTB office in London.

At all approved sites a camping pass is required and overseas visitors should have an International Camping Carnet. You can get a visitor's pass at the first site where you stay and this costs D kr 24 or D kr 48 for a family and is valid for a year.

Overnight prices depend on the site facilities but a typical charge is D kr 26 – 31 for an adult for 24 hours, with children half price. A few sites charge per 'unit' – that is per person, car or tent.

The Danish motoring organisation FDM also runs some 26 sites and these are open to foreign visitors holding an International Camping Carnet.

Camping at places other than designated sites in a tent, car or caravan is not allowed without the landowner's permission. Nor is it permitted to camp in car parks or lay-bys and strong measures are taken against anyone camping on sand dunes or the beach – offenders being fined on the spot.

FACILITIES FOR THE HANDICAPPED

Denmark, like its Scandinavian neighbours, has paid a great deal of attention to the needs of the disabled. There are numerous hotels which can accommodate the handicapped and some of the holiday centres have apartments with special facilities for the disabled. This also applies to Danish youth hostels, while the FDM (the Danish motoring organisation) has 10 camping sites suitable for disabled persons (their address is Blegdamsvej 124, DK-1200 Copenhagen Ø).

You can obtain details about suitable accommodation (and also museums, sights, etc., accessible to the handicapped) from Bolig-, Motor- og Hjælpemiddeludvalget, Hans Knudsens Plads 1A, DK-1200 Copenhagen Ø. For details of youth hostels catering for the handicapped write to Danmarks Vandrerhjem (address given earlier in this chapter).

Finally you can obtain helpful advice on this subject from the Danish Tourist Board's London office (see chapter on 'Useful Information').

FOOD AND DRINK

ONE OF THE pleasures of a holiday abroad should be the food, and in Denmark there is ample opportunity to enjoy the country's culinary specialities. The Danes are enthusiastic about food and therefore they pay a lot of attention to its preparation and serving.

Although mass production has made inroads in the catering field, just as in other countries, nevertheless there is still plenty of individuality and many dishes reflect the character of the country and its geographical position.

The raw materials that form the basis of Danish cuisine are, first and foremost, fish and shellfish, followed by meat, dairy products, vegetables and fruit. Many dishes are comparatively simple – in fact simplicity is the keynote – but because of the freshness of the raw materials they triumph. They take a lot of care with the table arrangements and the presentation of the dishes so that they are pleasing to the eye as well as exciting to the palate.

You only have to see a table prepared for some party or gala dinner to get the full measure of this art of presentation. It need not be a great event at some expensive restaurant in the capital; I have seen a table laid for a wedding party at a country inn and another, at a small seaside hotel, prepared for a local dinner and in both cases the table arrangements were a joy to behold. They only awaited the colour and animation of the guests and good food and drink to complete the picture.

Danish restaurateurs – at least many of them – believe that whatever the price of the dish it should involve the best ingredients. So you can always order a cheaper dish and know that the quality will be maintained. In my last dozen visits to Denmark I can only think of two or three dishes I have been offered which were below the best standard and only one that was really unacceptable. On the other hand I have, during the same period, visited several small restaurants where I did not expect to eat particularly well and have been surprised and delighted at the food presented to me.

OPEN SANDWICHES

The two best known elements of Danish cuisine are the open sandwich (*smørrebrød*) and the cold table (*Det Koldt Bord*). The most minor part of the open sandwich is the piece of bread and butter which forms the base. This may be white bread (*franskbrød*) or rye bread (*rugbrød*) and on top will be either fish, meat or cheese with salad, dressings or garnishes. The popular ones are herring (it may be marinated, pickled or in a curry sauce), roast beef, pork, ham, salami, liver paste, egg, fish (a small fish fillet), shrimps and cheese. All will be carefully garnished. Two open sandwiches will prove quite filling and if that isn't enough you can always have another one.

Smørrebrød is one of the best solutions for lunch: not too much and not too little and you determine how much you want either on the basis of quantity or price. (The cost of a sandwich varies from Dkr 6.50 to Dkr 45). You may think that some of them are expensive but when you see what has been artistically balanced on that little piece of bread you will realise they are good value. Obviously the more expensive ones are those with toppings of such things as fresh shrimps or smoked salmon.

Open sandwiches are a Danish institution and something you must try on your visit and nearly all restaurants and cafeterias offer them. In many cases you will be brought a long printed list and you mark on it the sandwiches you want, although this practice does seem to be dying out.

With your open sandwiches you can drink beer, and possibly have an aquavit (it goes particularly well with herring and the Danes say it gives the fish something in which to swim!). Or you can have soft drinks, or tea or coffee.

THE COLD TABLE

Basically the cold table is a help-yourself buffet with a wide variety of hot and cold dishes: fish, meat, vegetables, salads and garnishes plus sweets, cheese and fruit. But this is reducing it to a very prosaic level because when you see a really well presented cold table it is a mouth-watering work of art. Compared with a few years ago there are not so many restaurants offering this speciality and this may be due to people being more calorie conscious. You pay a fixed price and then help yourself to whatever you want – and, of course, as much as you want. Beer (plus aquavit for the herring) or soft drinks are the beverages to go with it.

There is an order of things when taking the cold table and you do not heap one plate willy-nilly with a glorious mixture. No, that is not the way to do it. You start with the herring, which is really the appetiser, then you can look at the other fish or maybe some Danish caviar. Then back to the table for another clean plate (use one for each 'course' – after all you aren't doing the washing up) and sample some cold meat with a salad or perhaps try the hot food. Then there is the delicious dessert (leave room for that) and conclude with some good Danish cheese and perhaps a little fruit. Finally, a cup of coffee and you are replete.

BREAKFAST

In nearly all hotels breakfast is now a help-yourself buffet. There is usually fruit juice and milk, cereal and oatmeal, a variety of rolls and bread, jam and marmalade, cheese and cold meat and tea or coffee. The more elaborate include a wider variety of meats, liver paste, herring and Danish pastries. Boiled eggs used to be fairly standard but they are now almost always an 'extra'. A small point: there is sometimes sour milk (buttermilk) as well as ordinary milk on the breakfast buffet. Don't confuse the two as it could add an unusual taste to your cornflakes.

SOME DANISH DISHES

Fish Fish dishes are the outstanding experience, being so fresh and of such high quality. Plaice is the basic fish, served steamed, fried in oil or butter 'a la meuniere' and garnished with vegetables and shellfish. Eel is another speciality which you can have fried with creamed potatoes and a white sauce or boiled with rice and a curry sauce. Shellfish are also splendid: lobsters, shrimps, mussels and oysters are all of exceptionally good quality. Equally good is the smoked salmon – the best comes from the island of Bornholm – served in fine slices with *surbrød* (bread made from rye meal and caraway seeds) or with spinach, scrambled egg or asparagus. Also the Scandinavian speciality called *Gravad laks* – salmon marinated with salt, sugar and dill and served with *surbrød* and a cold sauce of oil, mustard and sugar sprinkled with chopped dill.

Meat Danish meat is home-produced and of good quality although by contrast the bacon is nowhere near as good as that which is exported to the U K. A dish you will find on many menus is *Frikadeller* – a type of meat ball or rissole and made from freshly minced pork or pork and veal, flour, egg, salt, pepper and grated onions. It is often served with red cabbage, boiled potatoes and a thick brown gravy. It may not sound that exciting but it tastes delicious. Beef, pork and veal dishes are all good while lamb is more popular now than it was a few years ago. Poultry is usually either chicken or duck, while game is available in season.

Cheese There are quite a few domestic cheeses, apart from the widely known Danish blue (*Danablu*). They include *Castello* (white-veined), *Blå Castello* (blue-veined), *Mycella, Esrom, Danbo, Maribo, Havarti* and *Samsø* (all hard cheeses).

WHERE TO EAT AND DRINK

Places to eat and drink fall into different categories. Here are some of them:

Bar	Drinks of all kinds, including beer, wine and spirits.
Bistro	Usually a place for inexpensive meals of all kinds.
Bodega	Drinks but also serving light meals.
Cafe	Drinks and often light meals. Some are comparable to restaurants.
Cafeteria	Inexpensive self-service establishments offering simple hot and cold

	dishes, open sandwiches, etc., tea and coffee and various kinds of drinks.
Fiskerestaurant	Specialises in seafood but probably having some meat dishes on the menu.
Frokostrestaurant/ Frokoststue	Open sandwiches and small hot dishes.
Grillbar	Grilled beef, chicken, sausages, etc.
Hotel	Restaurants usually cover all meals from breakfast to late night snacks.
Konditori	Pastries and cakes, tea, coffee and soft drinks.
Kro	Inn, providing all kinds of food and drinks (may close on one day a week).
Motel	Facilities can vary from a bar, with possibly some light snacks, to a full-scale restaurant.
Pub	Drinks, with a greater emphasis on beer, and light meals such as open sandwiches.
Pølsevogn	A hamburger stand or kiosk, often found in a town square or similar location. Frankfurters and hamburgers.
Restaurant	All kinds of food and drinks.
Smørrebrødsforretning	Basically a take-away for open sandwiches. Frequently sells soft drinks. Quite often you can consume your sandwiches on the premises at a stand-up counter. Some of them keep open late and may have an automat outside for when they are closed.

Besides Danish restaurants there is a growing number of speciality restaurants offering the cuisine of other countries, such as French, Italian, Indian and Chinese. Pizzerias have become very common and there are the inevitable burger bars and the equally inevitable Macdonalds.

Opening hours vary but in general, restaurants are open from 12 noon to midnight (last orders for hot dishes normally 9.00 p.m. or 10.00 p.m.).

DANMENU

For those eating on a budget, look out for the *Danmenu* sign outside restaurants. The *Danmenu* is a two-course lunch or dinner served at a fixed price of D kr 75 including VAT and service. There are over 400 restaurants offering the *Danmenu,* although some only provide it at lunchtime while others only serve it in the evenings.

Some cafeterias offer a tourist menu and these exhibit a sign saying *Tourist Cafeteria Menu.* The meal consists of a main dish and a dessert.

DRINKS

Domestically produced alcoholic drinks include aquavit (schnapps), beer and liqueurs. There are different kinds of aquavit, some of which are flavoured with sweet myrtle, caraway or dill. They vary from being colourless to being pale gold but are always served well chilled.

Among the liqueurs the best known to the UK visitor is Peter Heering's cherry brandy, but there are others flavoured with coffee or blackcurrant for example. Then there are the bitters, the most widely drunk being *Gammel Dansk* which has the reputation for being a good hangover remedy.

The lightest beer, with the lowest alcohol content is *Lys pilsner* while lagers are referred to as either pilsner or lager (but more probably by the brand name, such as *Carlsberg Hof* or *Tuborg Grøn*). A stronger lager is *Eksport* or *Guldøl,* while draught beer is *fadøl* and in case you have not realised it already, the word for beer is *øl.* Stout is called *porter.*

Of course there is a considerable difference between the price you will pay for a bottle of beer in a supermarket and what it will cost when served to you in a restaurant. The much higher price of the latter reflects the cost of labour, plus VAT and service.

All wines are imported from France, Germany, Italy and Spain. *Åben vin, bordvin* or *husetsvin* stand for open, table and house wine respectively, and all basically describe a restaurant's house wine. Usually of a good standard it is more often presented in the bottle rather than in a carafe (when it may be referred to as *karaffelvin*). Wine lists will have a good selection of better wines but with prices to match. Types of wine are *Rosevin-* rosé, *rødvin* - red and *hvidvin* - white.

USEFUL TRANSLATIONS

Non-alcoholic drinks

Appelsin	orangeade
Cacao	chocolate
Citronvand	lemon soda
Dansk Vand	plain soda water
Kaffe	coffee
Kærnemælk	buttermilk
Letmælk	low fat milk
Mineralvand	mineral water/soda water

Mælk	milk
Skummetmælk	skim milk
Sødmælk	milk*
Te	tea
Tomatjuice	tomato juice
Vand	water
Æblemost	apple juice

* There are various kinds of cartoned milk, but this is the standard one for drinking, putting on your cereal or in your tea.

Menu terms

Børnemenu	children's menu
Dagens middag	set dinner
Dagens ret	dish of the day
Dampet	steamed
Desserter	desserts
Farseret/fyldt	stuffed
Fisk	fish
Filet	fillet (meat or fish)
Fjerkræ	poultry
Forretter	starter
Frisk	fresh
Friteret	deep fried
Frokost	lunch
Frugt	fruit
Gratineret	au gratin
Grillretter	grill dishes
Grillstegt	grilled
Grønsager	vegetables
Hovedretter	main dishes
Kogt	boiled
Kold	cold
Koldt Bord	cold table – help-yourself buffet
Kød	meat (dishes)
Mad	food
Mellemretter	side dishes
Morgenmad/ Morgencomplet	breakfast
Nat mad	late night snack
Osteanretning	cheeses
Pandestegt	cooked in a frying pan
Platte	a mini-cold table served on one large dish
Pocheret	poached
Salater	salads
Smørrebrød	open sandwiches

49

FOOD AND DRINK

Snitter	mini-open sandwiches – more like canapés
Steg	roast
Supper	soups
Varme retter	hot dishes

Food terms – fish and shellfish

Ferskrøget laks	lightly smoked salmon
Fiskeboller	fish balls
Forel	trout
Gravad laks	salmon marinated in salt, sugar and dill
Hellefisk	flounder
Helleflynder	halibut
Hummer	lobster
Jomfruhummer	Norwegian crayfish/scampi
Karry sild	herring in curry sauce
Krabbe	crab
Kryddersild	spiced pickled herring
Kuller	haddock
Laks	salmon
Marineret sild	marinated herring
Muslinger	mussels
Rejer	shrimps
Rødspætte	plaice
Rødtunge	lemon sole
Røget laks	smoked salmon
Sild	herring
Skaldyr	shellfish
Søtunge	sole
Østers	oysters
Ål	eel

Meat

Bajerske pølser	frankfurters/hot dogs
Bøf	beef steak
Crepinetter	pork or veal burgers
Engelsk bøf	steak and onions
Flæsk	pork
Fransk bøf	steak with parsley butter
Frikadeller	fried meatballs of pork or pork and veal
Grill pølse	grilled sausage
Hakkebøf	Danish-style beefburger
Helstegt højreb	roast saddle of beef
Helstegt lammeryg	roast saddle of lamb
Helstegt svinekam	roast loin of pork
Højrebskotelet	cutlet of prime rib of beef

50

Kalve filet	fillet of veal
Kødboller	meat balls
Lam	lamb
Lammekoteletter	lamb chops
Oksefilet	fillet of beef
Okseteg	roast beef
Pariserbøf	ground steak, lightly grilled both sides
Pølse	sausage
Ribbenssteg	roast rib of pork
Skinke	ham
Spegepølse	Danish salami

Poultry and Game

And	duck
Due	pigeon
Fasan	pheasant
Gås	goose
Høne	chicken (boiling fowl)
Kylling	chicken
Vildt	game

Cheese, eggs and cream

Blødkogt æg	soft boiled egg
Fløde	cream
Flødeskum	whipped cream
Hardkogt æg	hard boiled egg
Ost	cheese
Spejlæg	fried egg
Æg	egg
Æggekage	pan omelette
Røræg	scrambled egg

Vegetables

Agurk	cucumber
Asparges	asparagus
Bagt kartoffel	baked potato
Blomkål	cauliflower
Brasede kartofler/ Brasekartofler	saute potatoes
Bønner	beans
Franske kartofler	French fried potatoes
Grønkal	kale
Grønne ærter/ Grønærter	peas
Gulerod/Gulerødder	carrot
Hvide kartofler	boiled potatoes
Hvidkål	white cabbage
Kartofler	potatoes

51

FOOD AND DRINK

Løg	onion
Persille	parsley
Rosenkål	Brussel sprouts
Rødkål	red cabbage
Spinat	spinach
Surkål	sauerkraut
Ærter	peas

Fruit

Ananas	pineapple
Blommer	plum
Citron	lemon
Druer	grapes
Fersken	peach
Hindbær	raspberry
Jordbær	strawberry
Kirsebær	cherry
Nødder	nut
Pære	pear
Æble	apple

Various

Brød	bread
Butterdej	puff pastry
Flute	dinner roll
Franskbrød	white bread
Kager	cakes and pastries
Kiks	biscuits
Pandekager	pancakes
Postej	pâté
Ris	rice
Ristet brød	toast
Rugbrød	rye bread
Sennep	mustard
Smør	butter
Sukker	sugar
Vafler	waffle
Wienerbrød	Danish pastry

Selected dishes

Biksemad	fried sliced onion, meat and potatoes
Brændende Kærlighed	mashed potato with fried bacon and onions
Flæsekæggekage	pan omelette with bacon
Høkerpande	fried onion, meat, liver, kidney and potatoes
Lobescowes	stew of beef and potatoes
Skipperlabskous	Captain's stew – a traditional thick stew

SHOPPING

DENMARK IS a good country in which to shop, not because things are cheap, but because of the range of products and their quality. There are the traditional goods for which Denmark has a deservedly high reputation: porcelain and glass, silverware and pewter, jewellery, furniture and furs. But apart from these, there are other products which are worthy of attention.

So what should the visitor look for? There are those traditional products already mentioned, although in most cases you will want to rule out furniture (too bulky) or furs (unless you have a very deep pocket). Porcelain, glass, silverware and pewter – the Danes call it tin – need not be the designs produced by the top names (with prices to match). There are plenty of really stunning examples available in the lower price ranges. Jewellery – gold, silver and also incorporating precious and semi-precious stones – is very attractive and includes some beautiful work by gifted designers and craftsmen. You will find a remarkably wide range, even in small-town jewellers.

Other products worth looking into include leather (expensive, but good), knitwear (especially woollen sweaters), toys (think of Lego, that's Danish), textiles, ceramics and needlework. It is a good country in which to find things for the home or garden. Merchandise for the home includes both pretty things and those of a more utilitarian nature.

The Danes love candles and they come in all shapes and sizes and are a good buy. This also applies to attractive candle holders and table decorations. Ironmongery, tools and garden equipment are worth looking at, although some brands will be familiar.

Denmark has become something of an international fashion centre in recent years and this is reflected in the ladies wear available (especially casual clothes for the young). Some of the exciting designs are very competitively priced. Chocolate and confectionery shops offer mouth-watering and tempting goodies, which may not be cheap but will be of excellent quality.

What is enjoyable is that even quite small towns have an attractive range of shops, with a wide selection of beautifully displayed merchandise. As shops are nearly all individually-owned the monotony of high streets filled with multiples is avoided. With many towns having pedestrian precincts, shopping or just browsing is very pleasant.

There are no chain stores as we know them, except among supermarkets. There are also few department stores, these being restricted to the larger towns and Copenhagen. What is growing is the building of major shopping centres on the outskirts of the larger towns and cities. Taking Århus as an example, there is, on the outskirts, *City Vest* which incorporates two department stores and 65 specialist shops and *Bilka*, a discount centre which has 32 shops and a cafeteria. In the city there are two major department stores: *Salling* which has 34 departments on six floors, and a branch of *Magasin,* which is the biggest department store in Copenhagen.

Driving around the countryside it will become apparent that there are many artists' workshops: painters, sculptors, potters and so on. Visiting them can be rewarding the key being whether you like their style and prices. There are plenty of antique and bric-à-brac shops in towns and villages and some of these may have items to interest you, depending on what you collect.

If Danish food has appealed to you then you should include a last minute call at a food shop or supermarket before you catch your ferry to Britain. For example, what about some jars of herring, or Danish caviar or cheese. There are several supermarket chains, including *Føtex, Brugsen, Irma* and *Qvickly.*

Supermarkets are well laid out, scrupulously clean and often include a cafeteria and toilets. Parking will be close at hand. The big ones include other merchandise besides food and drink.

SHOPPING IN COPENHAGEN

For the visitor, shopping in the Danish capital tends to be concentrated on *Strøget,* the long pedestrian street that runs from the Town Hall Square to Kongens Nytorv. It is in fact five streets which just run into each other. Along Strøget you will find the top shops and famous names: Georg Jensen, Royal Copenhagen Porcelain, Bing and Grøndahl and Illum. But there are many smaller stores and good specialist shops and it now teems with boutiques stocked with exciting new fashions.

You should explore the smaller streets and squares leading off Strøget where you will find shops and boutiques full of new ideas and designs. In the streets towards the university quarter (and not far from Strøget) are secondhand and antiquarian bookshops, stamp dealers and antique shops. There are two other pedestrian streets worth a browse: Købmagergade and Filstræde.

On *Kongens Nytorv* is Magasin, the capital's biggest department store which has a useful gift department if you get stuck for ideas and are short of time.

Credit cards were slow to take off in Denmark but are now widely accepted, although perhaps not on the same scale as in the UK. You can also pay in most shops by Eurocheque or travellers' cheque. If you want cash, the banks are open from 9.30 a.m. to 4.00 p.m. Mondays to Fridays (6.00 p.m. on Thursdays) and are closed Saturdays, Sundays and bank holidays.

Shopping hours are usually 9.00 a.m. to 5.30 p.m. with late night shopping (9.00 a.m. to 7.00 p.m. or 8.00 p.m.) on Fridays. On Saturdays shops close at 1.00 p.m.(department stores at

2.00 p.m.). Some shops, particularly food shops, may close on Mondays. Outside normal hours you will find places open for the sale of tobacco, newspapers and confectionery. Bakeries, florists and *smørrebrødsforretning* (open sandwich take-aways) stay open for longer hours (bakers also open on Sundays). Some supermarkets have two late night openings a week, such as Thursdays to 7.00 p.m. and Fridays to 8.00 p.m. At the railway stations at Copenhagen, Århus and Ålborg there are supermarkets open every day of the week and the station kiosks stay open late in the evenings.

Danish shopkeepers have sales just like anywhere else and this may provide the opportunity to pick up a bargain. Look for the word *Udsalg* on the shop windows and then see what is on offer.

SHOPPING FOR FOOD

If you are self-catering or want to have picnics then you will need food. This presents no great problem and the easiest solution is undoubtedly the supermarket, either one of the major ones in a town or one of the mini-markets which will be found in villages. The larger supermarkets will have fresh food counters as well as packaged and frozen food. Most places seem to be able to find someone who has a few words of English if you get into difficulties, although sign language can achieve wonders. Instructions on packets pose more of a problem as misinterpretation could mean the difference between a good meal and a culinary disaster. Bakers provide a splendid range of bread, rolls and cakes and pastries, all deliciously fresh and appetising.

The open sandwich take-aways can solve the picnic problem in an instant. Just select the ones you want and you will get them neatly boxed. If a filling (or perhaps it should be called topping on an open sandwich) is not on display they can usually make it up for you. Many sandwich shops also sell soft drinks.

If you think you may be indulging in picnics – and they do free you from looking for a place to eat as well as saving money – remember to take some knives and forks (even plastic ones will do) as trying to eat open sandwiches in your fingers can be a messy business. A cold bag is also useful, although these and other picnic equipment will be found in profusion in Denmark.

There are lots of spacious lay-bys and pleasant areas for picnics. Quite a few have toilets and they nearly all have litter bins or sacks – so please use them and help to keep this pleasant little country neat and tidy.

ATTRACTIONS FOR CHILDREN AND ADULTS

IN SPITE of its modest size there is a multiplicity of things to see and do in Denmark. There are the simple visual pleasures of the scenery, the forests, the varied coastline, the lakes and streams. History provides a subject for many more attractions, ranging from the pre-historic, through the Viking era, the Middle Ages to more recent times.

The country is rich in castles and manor houses. The former are less forbidding and fortress-like than those found in Britain, but they are often impressive architecturally and are invariably sited in beautiful surroundings.

Museums abound, and these are not dry-as-dust affairs but places that really bring the past to life through the imaginative treatment of their exhibits. The Danes are experts in the creation of outdoor museums with old buildings painstakingly re-erected on suitable sites. Of course the Vikings play an important part in the attractions of historic interest, but other times also receive their fair share of attention. There are many museums devoted to the arts, while those concerned with specialist themes have subjects ranging from drifting sands to ships in bottles.

Architecture plays its part in things to see, as a great deal of pleasure can be gained from strolling round carefully preserved old buildings and streets which have received an enormous amount of care and attention.

Children are well catered for, starting with the two biggest attractions the country has to offer: Legoland and Tivoli Gardens. But there are many other sights and scenes that appeal to the younger visitor, from the simple (like a sandy beach) to the more mechanical (such as a veteran steam train).

A particularly Danish phenomenon is the Sommerland. These are individually owned activity parks where you pay an admission fee and then all the different attractions can be enjoyed any number of times without further charge. Sommerlands have all sorts of things: boats, go-carts, trampolines, pony rides, aerial cableways – the list is very extensive. They are kept remarkably clean and tidy and have reasonably priced – and good – catering facilities or you are welcome to take your own picnic (you can even use their barbecues). For children they are wonderful, even if they are not quite as much fun for adults – but they do offer value for money and make a good day out for the family.

In this chapter I include a broad range of attractions, but of course there are many more and some of these are referred to in the individual itineraries. In most cases I have given an indication of when museums, etc., are open, but these are often subject to adjustment. Check with the Danish Tourist Board's London office or with the appropriate local tourist office. Remember that many attractions are only open daily in the summer season; at other times they may be open only at weekends or not at all.

Expect to pay an entrance fee at nearly all museums, castles and so on. Parking is always free and you can expect to find clean toilets; if catering facilities are provided these will be hygienic and inviting.

The arrangement here is geographical, i.e. Jutland, Funen, and so on. In the case of Jutland I have started in the south near the German frontier and progressed to the northern tip of the peninsula. Those places marked with a ☆ should be of interest to children, while the numbers identify the attractions on the accompanying map.

JUTLAND

1 Tønder Close to the German border and a former centre of the lace-making industry. Has a well-preserved 17th–18th century townscape with many houses having unusual painted doorways. Excellent museum which covers this southern part of Jutland. OPEN ALL YEAR, NOT MONDAYS IN WINTER.

2 Møgeltønder A beautifully preserved village street, tree-lined and cobbled. runs from the church at one end to the Schackenborg Palace at the other.

3 Sønderborg A busy town on the island of Als (a bridge away from Jutland). Imposing castle which today houses the largest museum outside Copenhagen. OPEN ALL YEAR.

4 Dybbøl Banke Just outside Sønderborg, on Jutland, and associated with the Danish-German war of 1864, has now become a national monument. The finely-restored Dybbøl windmill has a small museum and is a national symbol.

5 Haderslev It was in the cathedral – the tallest church in Scandinavia – that the message of reform by Martin Luther was first preached in Denmark. Museum of local history with an open air display of buildings. OPEN MAY – SEPT, CLOSED MONDAYS. In the riding school of the Holstein Lancers is the Schleswig Carriage Collection (*Slesvigske Vognsamling*) of carriages and sleighs from the period 1870 - 1930. OPEN IN JULY AND AUGUST.

6 Christiansfeld Founded in 1773 by the Moravian Brethren. The Brethren built a small town with a simple but completely harmonious architectural style. Museum, church – with plain whitewashed interior and no altar or pulpit.

7 Rømø Island off the west coast of Jutland (10½ miles long and three miles wide) and reached by a six-mile long causeway. Has some splendid beaches. Museum (*Nationalmuseets Kommandørgård*) at Toftum in the former 18th century home of a prosperous commander of the whaling fleet which shows how the owner would have lived.

ATTRACTIONS FOR CHILDREN AND ADULTS

8 Ribe Denmark's oldest market town with a medieval centre. Beautifully preserved little streets and buildings – the current preservation project involves 560 buildings. Splendid five-aisled Cathedral. Access to the tower at certain times with rewarding views of the surrounding area. Hans Tausen's House – residence of the Bishop of Ribe in 1541 – is now an archaeological museum. *Queden's Gård,* a four-winged half-timbered merchants' house, *c.*1580, is now a very interesting museum of interiors. OPEN ALL YEAR EXCEPT MONDAYS.

9 Mandø Small island off the Jutland coast which can be reached at low tide by a 'tractor bus'. Little church and museum.

10 Fanø The island facing Esbjerg. Eleven miles long and reached by ferry (20 mins). Superb beaches on the west coast. Distinctive seaman's church (*Nordby Kirke*) with ship models. Fanø museum is in a former seaman's home and includes the mementoes he brought back from his sailing ship voyages. OPEN SUMMER ONLY. Shipping and costume museum (*Fanø Søfarts og Dragtudstilling*) at Nordby. Sønderho, very pretty little village with distinctive thatched cottages.

11 Esbjerg Busy port of entry from Britain. Fisheries and Maritime Museum (*Fiskeri og Søfartsmuseet*). ☆ Has a unique collection of fishing gear from the past, also models of fishing boats. The saltwater aquarium has 200 species of fish found in Danish waters. Adjoining it is the sealarium. OPEN ALL YEAR. Art Pavilion – collection of contemporary Danish art. OPEN ALL YEAR. Printing Museum. OPEN MAY – SEPT. Town museum.

12 Varde Sommerland – amusement and activity park. ☆ Bowling, shooting gallery, climbing towers, trampolines, swings, see-saws, pony rides, boats, pedal cars, crazy golf, etc. OPEN 21 MAY – 31 AUG. Varde Miniby – the town in miniature, as it was in 1800. Museum.

13 Kolding Koldinghus Castle was a royal residence for centuries but was set on fire in 1808 and since 1900 it has been under reconstruction. Now a museum of cultural history and applied art. OPEN ALL YEAR. Geographical Garden and rose garden with more than 2,000 different varieties of trees and shrubs and 100 varieties of roses. OPEN ALL YEAR. Trapholt – new and impressive art museum. OPEN ALL YEAR.

14 Legoland, Billund ☆ Second biggest attraction in Denmark. Fantastic models in landscaped surroundings made from 26 million Lego bricks. Also Legocopters, traffic school, miniboats, thrilling timber ride, mini-train and mine train, Lego cars, Legoredo (wild west town), Indian camp (dig for gold), pony rides, Fabuland (for younger children), Legotop, a 118 ft high revolving tower. Indoor attractions include doll collection, old mechanical toys, Titania's palace, puppet theatre. OPEN 29 APR – 17 SEPT. Automobile and aircraft museum adjoining Billund airport opens in 1990.

15 Jelling Ancient seat of Danish royalty. King Gorm the old and Queen Thyre are believed to be buried in one of the two huge burial mounds. In the churchyard are the runic stones, one of which has the oldest depiction of Christ in a relief surrounded by animal ornamentation. Church has 12th century frescoes.

16 Lions Park, Givskud *(Løveparken)* ☆ Safari park with 700 animals, including 40 lions. OPEN 29 APR – 27 SEPT.

17 Vejle Attractive fjord location. The southern arm of the fjord is particularly beautiful and rises steeply through beech woods (321 ft above sea level) to Munkebjerg.

18 Glud Small village with an interesting museum of Danish bygones and several old buildings, complete with interiors. Old implements and artefacts.

19 Ringkøbing Market town, six miles from the west coast and having a number of little streets and old buildings. At the local airport at Stauning is a veteran aircraft museum which includes Denmark's oldest plane in a flyable condition.

20 Sommerland West, Hee About five miles north of Ringkøbing. ☆ Covers an area of 55 acres. Attractions include mini-train, go-carts, giant air cushion, rowing boats, aerial cableway, canoes, pony rides and Vikingland (at which children can participate in old skills). OPEN 1 MAY – 21 AUG.

21 Holstebro Museum and art gallery with contemporary Danish art and graphics by foreign artists. OPEN DAILY, EXCEPT MONDAYS. Impressive range of sculptures and fountains in different parts of the town. Dragoons and Freedom Museum (*Dragon og Frihedsmuseet*). OPEN WEEKDAY AFTERNOONS 1 MAY – 30 SEPT.

22 Herning Ancient settlement now a modern commercial town. Modern art collection and sculpture park. Unusual setting for contemporary art. OPEN ALL YEAR, CLOSED MONDAYS. Herning Museum includes an appealing series of little dioramas depicting life in the past throughout the seasons.

23 Bryrup-Vrads Preserved railway which runs through delightful rural scenery. ☆ WEEKENDS IN SUMMER.

24 Silkeborg Town in the centre of the Danish lake district. Museum, in the town's oldest building, includes the preserved head of the Tollund Man – 2,200 years old. ☆ OPEN ALL YEAR. Art museum includes an exhibition of Asger Jorns work, the

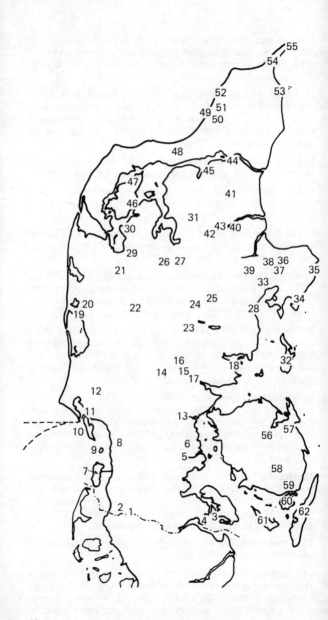

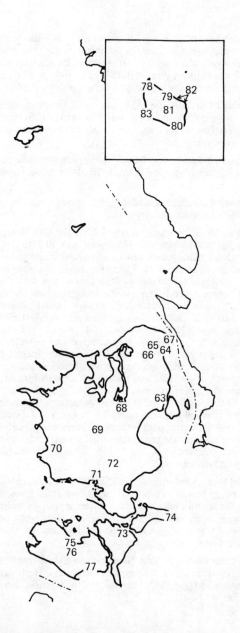

Cobra group and modern European art. OPEN DAILY, EXCEPT MONDAYS. An area of attractive scenery including Himmelbjerget (*'Heavenly Mountain'*) 426 ft above sea level. On the summit is an 82 ft high tower, erected in 1875. The 1861 paddle steamer *'Hjejlen'* is among the vessels providing trips on the lakes.

25 Jutland Car Museum *(Jysk Automobil Museum)*, **Gjern** ☆ An interesting and expanding collection of over 130 beautifully restored old motor vehicles. OPEN DAILY IN SUMMER, WEEKENDS 1 – 30 APR AND 15 SEPT – 31 OCT.

26 Mønsted Limestone Mines ☆ Impressive underground galleries the deepest of which are 114 ft below ground. OPEN APR – OCT.

27 Viborg Cathedral, founded 1130; present building dates from 1876. Pleasant park by a lake.

28 Århus Denmark's second largest city. The Old Town (*Den Gamle By*) is a fascinating collection of over 60 17th and 18th century town buildings – houses, shops, workshops and so on – from all over Denmark. ☆ OPEN ALL YEAR. Museum of pre-history, Moesgård (*Forhistorisk Museum*) occupies a delightful setting between woods and water. Exhibits include the 2,000-year-old 'Grauballe Man'. OPEN ALL YEAR, CLOSED MONDAYS MID SEPT – END MAR. Cathedral, late gothic and the longest church in Denmark. Town Hall, completed 1941. Conducted tours in summer; the tower can also be ascended and provides good views of the city and Århus bay. Concert hall, opened 1982. Superb facilities and an imposing piece of modern architecture with several stages, café and restaurant. Danish Fire Brigade Museum. ☆ Biggest collection of fire fighting appliances in the world. OPEN APR – END OCT. Århus Aquarium, Tranbjerg. ☆ Rare fish from all over the world. OPEN ALL YEAR. Tivoli Friheden. ☆ Amusement park with among other things, the biggest roller-coaster and oldest roundabout in Denmark. Marselisborg Forest and Deer Park – a beautiful recreation area on the edge of the city and by the water.

29 Hjerl Hede, Vinderup ☆ Near Skive. 2,500 acres of National Trust land by Lake Flyndersø, part of which is devoted to a large scale open air museum. Many different kinds of buildings, also stone age settlement and forestry and peat digging museums. Surroundings are heather clad hills and forests of oak and pine. OPEN 1 APR – 31 OCT.

30 Spøttrup Castle, Balling. Nearest town Skive. One of Denmark's finest medieval castles. Double moats. Herb garden. OPEN DAILY 1 MAY – 23 OCT; 1 – 30 APR ON SUNDAYS AND BANK HOLIDAYS.

31 Denmark's Bicycle Museum, Ålestrup ☆ About 100 bicycles, also some early sewing machines and radios. OPEN 1 MAY – 31 OCT, CLOSED MONDAYS.

32 Samsø Pretty little island largely unspoiled, reached by car ferry from Hov (east Jutland) or Kalundborg (Zealand). Picturesque villages, particularly Ballen and Nordby. Interesting museum (*Samsø Museumsgård*) with interiors and housed in an old farmhouse.

33 Rosenholm Castle, Hornslet This renaissance building dates back to 1559 and has an impressive interior which includes 300-year-old Flemish tapestries. Beautiful gardens. CONDUCTED TOURS 25 JUNE – 7 AUG; PARK OPEN AT OTHER TIMES.

34 Ebeltoft Attractive little town and a popular holiday centre and with a number of old streets with half-timbered buildings. Frigate *'Jylland'* ☆ is the oldest preserved wooden ship in Denmark. OPEN MAY – OCT. Doll Museum ☆ with over 500 dolls. OPEN IN SUMMER.

35 Grenå Town with ferry harbour. Djursland Museum, housed in old half-timbered building in the town centre.

36 Djurs Sommerland, Nimtofte Very good and imaginative activity park between Randers and Grenå. ☆ Mini-golf, bowling, giant playground, rifle range, archery, pony rides, wild west town, rowing and paddle boats, mini-trains, go-carts, giant sandpit, cable slide, giant chute, mini-zoo and trampolines are just some of the attractions. OPEN 12 MAY – 28 AUG.

37 Djursland Railway Museum, Ryomgård ☆ Small exhibits, uniforms and models and housed in the railway station building. RATHER RESTRICTED OPENING HOURS BETWEEN MARCH AND NOV.

38 Gammel Estrup, Auning Renaissance castle founded *c.* 1500 and rebuilt and enlarged 1600 - 1630. Now a manor house museum. An agricultural museum is housed in the former farm buildings. OPEN DAILY MAY – OCT; RESTRICTED OPENING NOV – APR.

39 Clausholm Castle, Voldum A five-winged mansion built in simple baroque style in 1699 - 1723. Interesting interiors, while the chapel has Denmark's oldest organ. Grounds with terraces and fountains. OPEN DAILY MID-MAY – MID-SEPT.

40 Mariager-Handest Veteran Railway ☆ Interesting collection of locomotives, railcars and rolling stock from Danish private railways. RUNS SUNDAYS, JUNE – AUG. Mariager is also a charming little town.

41 Rebild Hills Splendid hilly area with the nearby *Rold Skov,* the largest forest area in Denmark. The Rebild Hills (*Rebild*

Bakker) form a national park donated by Danish-Americans in 1912. Lincoln log cabin includes an emigrants' museum and nearby is a museum of local history and folk music. At Thingbæk are former limestone mines which now house more than 100 works by the noted Danish sculptors Anders Bundgård and C.J. Bonnesen.

42 Klejtrup Sø (lake), near Hobro ☆ Map of the world (scale 10.6 in equals 68.9 miles) partly dug out of the shore and partly built out into the lake. OPEN MAY – SEPT.

43 Fyrkat, near Hobro Mound of a Viking Ring Fort, *c.* 1,000. Viking house under reconstruction. OPEN ALL YEAR, CLOSED MONDAYS.

44 Ålborg Large commercial city on the Limfjord. St. Budolfi Cathedral, built in the Middle Ages. Large altar piece, carved pulpit and carillon of 48 bells. Holy Ghost Monastery (*Helligåndsklostret*). Cloisters from 1431 with interesting historical collection. Impressive merchants' houses: Jens Bang's House (1624) the largest Renaissance building in Scandinavia; and Jørgen Olufsen's House (1616). Interesting restored townscape with old buildings. Ålborg Historical Museum has a stone age collection. OPEN ALL YEAR. North Jutland Museum of Art includes works by both Danish and international artists. OPEN ALL YEAR, CLOSED MONDAYS, EXCEPT IN SUMMER. Ålborg Zoo. ☆ More than 1,500 animals. OPEN ALL YEAR. Ålborg Tower, Skovbakken, 344 ft above sea level. Magnificent views. OPEN APR – SEPT. Tivoliland. ☆ Large amusement park with 80 attractions. OPEN APR – SEPT. Lindholm Høje, near Ålborg. Biggest burial place in Scandinavia dating back to the Germanic iron age and Viking period. 700 graves. OPEN ALL YEAR. Vandland - northern Europe's largest sub-tropical aquatic activity park. OPEN ALL YEAR.

45 Nibe Best preserved little town of its period in the area of the Limfjord. Old buildings and narrow streets. Founded on fishing for herring, now a quiet backwater.

46 Jesperhus Flower Park, Mors (near Nykøbing) Scandinavia's largest flower garden with 500,000 plants. Also an aquarium and attractions for children. OPEN 15 MAY – 20 SEPT.

47 Hanklit, on the island of Mors Cliffs 200 ft high of Moler clay and with layers of black volcanic ash.

48 Fjerritslev Brewery Museum - housed in a former country brewery.

49 Blokhus-Løkken A broad stretch of sandy beach backed by sandhills. The sand is so firm that you can drive on it the entire distance from Blokhus to Løkken.

50 Fårup Sommerland, Saltum ☆ The pioneer activity park in Denmark. Includes canoeing, sailing, mini-golf, aerial ride, trampolines, pony rides, huge play area and 20,000 sq ft of air cushions. Opened in 1989 was a huge Aquapark. Park covers 20 acres. OPEN 12 MAY – 28 AUG.

51 Børglum Monastery A massive, and rather forbidding, building on a hilltop. Episcopal residence 1150 - 1530. The garden, church, baptistry and recently restored Gothic organ are open to the public. OPEN 1 MAY – 31 AUG.

52 Rubjerg Knude, near Lønstrup Nature reserve with large sand drifts and steep cliffs rising 240 ft from the sea. The lighthouse, now closed, is completely dwarfed by the sandhills and is a sand drift museum.

53 Frederikshavn International ferry port. The Gun Tower (*Krudttårnsmuseet*) built 1686 - 90 as part of the fortifications is now a museum of weapons and uniforms. Bangsbo Museum (on the outskirts of the town) is a fascinating and well-arranged museum relating to Frederikshavn and district, housed in a manor house and farm buildings. Includes an incredible collection of items made from human hair. Separate buildings are devoted to shipping (some splendid models), the occupation of Denmark in World War 2 and the activities of the Danish resistance movement. Also a Viking ship and a display of old horse carriages and agricultural implements. OPEN ALL YEAR, CLOSED SATURDAYS/SUNDAYS 1 NOV – 31 MAR. Cloostårnet, a 196 ft high tower (525 ft above sea level) offers spectacular views over the surrounding area. Lift. OPEN 1 MAY – 30 SEPT.

54 Råbjerg Mile An impressive migrating sand dune 875 yards wide by 1¼ miles long. Like a little bit of the Sahara in Denmark.

55 Skagen Northernmost town in Jutland and a great favourite with Danish artists, because of the quality of the light. The Skagen Museum contains many works from the golden age of Danish painting. OPEN DAILY 1 APR – 31 OCT AND SATURDAYS/ SUNDAYS 1 NOV – 31 MAR. Open air museum (*Skagen Fortidsminder*) includes old houses, windmill and also a fisheries museum. Distinctive ochre-coloured houses in the older part of the town. Beyond Skagen is Grenen, at the very tip of Jutland where the waters of the *Kattegat* meet the *Skagerrak*. You can walk over the sandhills to the point or ride a tractor train.

FUNEN
56 Odense third largest city in Denmark and the birthplace of Hans Christian Andersen. The H.C. Andersen Museum ☆ tells the story of his life and includes many of his personal belongings. OPEN ALL YEAR. His childhood home forms another museum.

ATTRACTIONS FOR CHILDREN
AND ADULTS

OPEN ALL YEAR. Danish State Railway Museum. ☆ Locomotives, coaches, models and relics from Denmark's railways of the past. OPEN DAILY 18 APR – 30 SEPT, SUNDAYS OCT – APR. Funen Village. An open air museum ☆ with old Funen buildings - houses, cottages, farms, mill, school, etc. OPEN DAILY APR – OCT, SUNDAYS NOV – MAR. Falck Museum. ☆ Collection of fire engines and emergency vehicles. OPEN DAILY (EXCEPT MONDAYS) MAY – OCT. Fyns Tivoli. ☆ Funfair, rides, etc. OPEN APR – AUG. St. Canutes Cathedral (*Sct. Knudskirke*), Denmark's most significant Gothic church building. Brandts Klædefabrik, cultural centre incorporating graphic and photographic museums, also art gallery. Museum on the life and work of composer Carl Nielsen, Museum of Cultural and Urban History.

57 Ladby Viking Ship *(Ladby skibet)*, **near Kerteminde** This Viking ship, *c.* 900, was a chief's grave.

58 Egeskov Castle and Veteran Transport Museum, Kværndrup ☆ One of the loveliest Renaissance castles to be found anywhere in Europe. Built 1524 - 54 in a lake on a foundation of oak piles. Beautiful park, museum of veteran cars and aircraft. OPEN DAILY 1 MAY – 30 SEPT.

59 Svendborg The oldest house in the town, Anne Hvides Gård (1560), is now part of the Svendborg and district museum. Sct. Nicolaj Church built *c.* 1200 in Romanesque style. Veteran ship *'Helge'* makes sightseeing trips FROM 6 JUNE – 14 AUG.

60 Tåsinge A charming island facing Svendborg across the Sound and linked by a bridge. One of Denmark's best preserved villages is Troense. Maritime museum with many interesting objects. Valdemars Castle, near Troense, occupies a beautiful position. At Bregninge you can climb the church tower and enjoy superb views of the surrounding area. Opposite the church is a Tåsinge 'skipper's home' and folk museum. At Vornæs is the Danish mechanical doll museum OPEN FRI, SAT, SUN MAY – AUG, DAILY 18 JUNE – 7 AUG.

61 Ærø One of the most beautiful islands in Denmark. Off the coast of Funen and reached by ferry from Svendborg, Fåborg, Rudkøbing or Mommark. Ærøskøbing the capital is *the* fairytale town with its old-world atmosphere, narrow cobbled streets and beautifully preserved little houses. Ærø Museum is a regional museum in the old pharmacy. OPEN JUNE – AUG. Hammerick's House with faience, furniture and tiles. OPEN JUNE – AUG. Ships in bottles museum. OPEN MAY – SEPT. Marstal, the other town on the island, was famous in the days of sail. Jens Hansen's Maritime Museum recalls the sailing ship era and has many maritime artefacts and over 40 ship models. OPEN APRIL – AUGUST. Marstal Church (1737) has six ship models hanging in the nave and the altar piece is unusual as the faces of the apostles are those of local skippers, long since deceased.

62 Langeland Long, thin island (32 miles by 7 miles) reached by bridge from Tåsinge. At Tranekær is the imposing red-painted Tranekær Castle beside the Borresø lake (park open to the public). Rudkøbing, the principal town, has many old houses.

ZEALAND

63 Copenhagen Places of interest in the Danish capital are dealt with in the chapter on Copenhagen and therefore the references here are restricted to two attractions outside the city centre; also one in the city centre: Tivoli Gardens. ☆ The most popular attraction in Denmark, there is no other amusement park in the world quite like it. Opened in 1843 'for the amusement of the people' it has continued to do just that ever since. OPEN 27 APRIL – 11 SEPT. Funfair, theatre, entertainments of all kinds, open air stage, gardens, fountains and fireworks and a unique atmosphere. Twenty-two restaurants. Not to be missed.

Bakken ☆ is another pleasure park only a few minutes by train or car from the city centre. Variety of entertainments: funfair, dance hall, restaurants and open air theatre. OPEN APR – END AUG. Open air museum (*Frilandsmuseet*) Sorgenfri, Lyngby in the Copenhagen suburbs. ☆ A whole range of old Danish buildings have been re-erected on the spacious 40 acre site. The interiors provide an insight into Danish rural life 100 years ago. OPEN DAILY, EXCEPT MONDAYS.

64 Louisiana, Humlebæk On the coast between Copenhagen and Helsingør. A most impressive and beautifully sited museum of modern art and a cultural centre. Extensive permanent collection plus regular exhibitions. OPEN ALL YEAR.

65 Fredensborg Palace, Fredensborg Built in the Italian style and early 18th century. A residence of the Danish Royal Family. Part of the palace is open in July while the extensive park is open all year.

66 Frederiksborg Castle, Hillerød This Renaissance castle built 1600–21 now houses the National Historical Museum which makes a fine setting for the furniture, paintings and portraits illustrating Denmark's past. About 70 rooms can be seen including the Knights' Hall, the Audience Chamber and the Chapel. The latter has a Compenius organ from 1610. OPEN ALL YEAR.

67 Helsingør Kronborg Castle, an impressive building which was the setting for Shakespeare's 'Hamlet'. Magnificent Great Hall while the King's and Queen's apartments are most noteworthy. The Chapel still looks as it was in 1582. There is a separate Mercantile and Maritime Museum with 27 rooms on Danish Colonial History, Shipbuilding, Navigation, Lights and Buoys

Service. The Casemates are noteworthy. OPEN ALL YEAR.
Denmark's Technical Museum. ☆ History of natural science
and technology with 2,000 items of everyday use. OPEN ALL
YEAR. Separate Traffic Department at another location, with vintage cars, bicycles, motor-cycles, etc OPEN ALL YEAR.
Helsingør-Gilleleje Veteran Railway. ☆ Offers a very pleasant
run in vintage coaches hauled by a steam locomotive. OPERATING
SUNDAYS JUNE – SEPT.

68 Roskilde Impressive 12th century cathedral, the Danish
equivalent of Westminster Abbey. Some 38 kings and queens are
entombed in the cathedral in splendid and varied sarcophagi.
Viking Ship Museum. ☆ Houses five Viking ships from the 11th
century which were recovered from the Roskilde Fjord. The
actual work of restoration takes place in the museum. Also much
background material relating to Viking ships, etc. OPEN ALL
YEAR. At the Lejre Research Centre (*Lejre Forsøgscenter*) near
Roskilde is an experimental reconstruction of an Iron Age settlement ☆ with buildings, workshops, tools and so on. It may sound
dull but it is, in fact, very fascinating. OPEN 1 MAY – 28 SEPT.

69 Skjoldenæsholm, Jystrup Tram Museum ☆ with operating
vintage trams from former Danish tramways. OPEN MAY – OCT
WEEKENDS, ALSO TUE, WED, THUR IN PEAK SUMMER.

70 Trelleborg, near Slagelse Impressive fortified Viking camp,
partly reconstructed. OPEN 1 APR – 30 SEPT.

71 Næstved Gavnø Manor, A Rococo palace (1755 - 58). Interiors and art collection. Chapel. OPEN ALL YEAR. Sparresholm
Carriage Collection, near Næstved, has a collection of carriages
and horse-drawn vehicles. OPEN SATS AND SUNS 12 MAY – 7
AUG. Also near Næstved is the Holmegård Glassworks at Fensmark. Demonstrations of glass blowing. OPEN ALL YEAR.

72 Gisselfeld Castle, near Haslev Renaissance Castle built in
1554 and later twice rebuilt. Set in one of Denmark's most
beautiful parks, laid out in English style, and extending to over
100 acres. Includes a lime tree planted by King Edward VII in
1904. OPEN 27 MAR – 31 AUG.

FALSTER

73 Stubbekøbing Motorcycle and Radio Museum Largest collection of veteran motorcycles in northern Europe. Also vintage
radios and gramophones. OPEN JUNE – AUG.

MØN

74 Møns Klint Fascinating chalk formations on the east coast of
the island of Møn. The cliffs rise to a height of 420 ft above sea
level and the highest point is the *'Dronningestolen'* (Queen's

Chair). Liselund, a short drive from the cliffs, has a romantic little Empire style thatched chateau, called the Danish *'Petit Trianon'* and built in 1795. Set in a beautiful park in which are three 18th century summerhouses: the Chinese House, the Norwegian House, and the Swiss Cottage.

LOLLAND

75 Knuthenborg Safari Park ☆ Between Maribo and Bandholm. Europe's biggest manorial park with 500 different species of trees and shrubs while the safari park has more than 700 animals. OPEN MAY – SEPT.

76 Maribo-Bandholm Veteran Railway ☆ Operates vintage trains at summer weekends.

77 Ålholm Castle, Nysted Much extended castle with one wing open to the public. The 62 acre park contains many different species of trees. OPEN 28 MAY – 31 AUG. The Ålholm Automobil Museum ☆ which lies to the west of the castle contains a fine collection of over 200 veteran and vintage cars. A train in the style of the 1850's links the museum with the seaside. OPEN WEEKENDS 16 APR – 11 OCT (DAILY 28 MAY – 31 AUG).

BORNHOLM

78 Hammershus Denmark's largest castle ruin, impressively located on a rocky plateau overlooking the sea. OPEN ALL YEAR.

79 Østerlars The largest round church on Bornholm (a distinctive feature of the island). Dates back to the 12th century. OPEN 15 APR – 1 OCT, EXCEPT SUNDAYS.

80 Dueodde Has a beach of very fine white sand. Lighthouse 153 ft high with a top platform which can be reached by climbing 196 steps. Magnificent views over the island from the top.

81 Almindingen Denmark's third largest forest. At Rytterknægten, within the forest, is the highest point on the island (530 ft above sea level) with an observation tower.

82 Gudhjem and Svaneke Two of the most delightful little towns on the island with small harbours and picturesque buildings.

83 Rønne Principal town on Bornholm with some attractive little streets and buildings. Very interesting museum devoted to the island's history and culture.

> *Note: General literature issued by the Danish Tourist Board and brochures published by the various regional tourist offices provide additional information on places of interest and current times of opening.*

SPORTS AND RECREATIONS

Swimming and bathing With 4,500 miles of coastline Denmark provides plenty of opportunities for swimming and bathing. There are many miles of fine beaches, frequently backed by sandhills. The west coast of Jutland has the longest stretches of sandy beach, but of course it faces the North Sea where you are more than likely to encounter windy conditions.

A more placid environment will be found on the east Jutland coast and around the islands of Funen and Zealand. There are quite a few good beaches which shelve gently into the water which makes them very safe for children. On the island of Bornholm you will find both a rocky coastline and areas with beautiful fine white sand.

All beaches are open freely to the public and none has been 'developed' as in so many other countries. At only a few places is bathing not allowed and this is usually around harbours. Nude bathing is permitted on many parts of the coast and topless bathing and sunbathing is commonplace.

If sea bathing does not appeal then you will find plenty of excellent public swimming pools while many hotels and holiday centres have indoor or outdoor pools.

Fishing With its extensive coastline, and plenty of well-stocked rivers and lakes, Denmark is a splendid country for the angler. For sea fishing there are numerous harbours where you can go out with an experienced local boatman and enjoy some really good sport. Off-shore fishing is allowed from virtually all stretches of the shore accessible to the public. Check with the local tourist office for information on the best places to go.

Freshwater fishing is very good and Denmark has an excellent reputation with British anglers. Rivers in Jutland are probably the best. Fishing rights are nearly always in private hands but are often let to local angling clubs. These clubs issue day cards (around Dkr 20–40) or weekly cards (about Dkr 75–100) to visitors. Local tourist offices frequently issue licences and can provide details of local angling opportunities. Addresses of Danish angling societies can be obtained from *Danmarks Sportsfiskerforbund, Worsaaesgade 1, DK-7100 Vejle.*

Sailing Danish waters are ideal for sailing and there are something like 600 harbours plus many well-equipped marinas. There are both open and sheltered waters and there are few places around the country where you cannot enjoy sailing. The area around south Funen and on the Limfjord are both sheltered and very attractive.

Boats of all kinds can be hired, but rates are generally higher than in the UK. Examples of one week hire charges are as follows: Sailing boat from Dkr 2,000, motor boat from Dkr 2,000 and motor sailer from Dkr 3,100. Prices are naturally lower outside the peak season.

On a smaller scale, there are opportunities for canoeing on several rivers, the best one being the Gudenå in Jutland. Typical cost of one day's canoeing (two seat canoe) is Dkr 150 and this includes the return transport of the canoe back to the hiring point.

Golf This has become an increasingly popular leisure pursuit in Denmark. From having only a handful of golf courses 20 years ago, there are now 60 courses, about half of which are 18-hole. Visiting golfers are welcome and all you need is your club membership card. Green fees are modest: weekdays Dkr 80-120, weekends and bank holidays Dkr 100-250. Details of golf courses, opening times, etc., are available from *Dansk Golf Union, Toftevej 26, DK-2625 Vallensbæk.*

Riding The number of horses and ponies in Denmark has increased at a surprising rate over the last few years. Consequently there are plenty of opportunities to ride and there is also plenty of enjoyable riding country. There are many riding schools with animals suitable for beginners or experts and for children or adults. Charges are broadly the same as those in Britain and a typical example is Dkr 45-60 per hour.

There are some riding holidays available and also riding camps for young people on Jutland and Funen. You can also hire a horse-drawn prairie wagon on Funen, Langeland and Samsø.

An interesting riding centre on Jutland is Bakholm which is devoted entirely to the distinctive Iceland horses which are full of character. You can have lessons, go for rides and they offer simple, homely accommodation where you can immerse yourself in a really horsey atmosphere. The centre is on the beautiful Djursland peninsula, about 12 miles from Grenå and 25 miles from Århus. The address is *Bakholm, Stabrandvej 3, DK-8560 Kolind.*

Various There are many other activities which can involve the visitor. Here are just a few: archaeology, botany, bird-watching, cycling, ceramics, dyeing, drawing, lace-making, painting, tennis, walking, weaving and windsurfing.

Meet the Danes In Århus and Odense there is a scheme in operation that lets you meet a local Danish family. You visit them in their home and have an opportunity to learn more about everyday life in Denmark. Contact the tourist office.

THE ITINERARIES – AN INTRODUCTION

ALL THE ROUTES in the itineraries have been personally checked, with one or two minor exceptions. In certain instances I have given what might be called a simplified route when suggesting minor roads. An examination of a good map will show that more complex – and perhaps more interesting – routes can be followed if you have the time (and the ability to read a map).

I have suggested overnight stops and have also recommended those centres where you should stay more than one night so you can do some additional sightseeing. These extra nights can be eliminated if you cannot spare the time.

In the chapter 'Attractions for Children and Adults' the various entries are numbered and, where these are also referred to in the itineraries, they are cross-referenced with the same number. You should refer to these entries as this information is not necessarily repeated in the itineraries. In the same way, any attractions for children are indicated with a ☆.

Those hotels, inns or restaurants which I have visited will often merit rather more description than those which are merely listed for general information purposes. The listed ones may be perfectly satisfactory, but it is simply a case of having no personal knowledge of them.

I would also issue the same word of caution that I have expressed elsewhere that many attractions, museums and so on are only open in summer or may have very limited opening hours for the rest of the year. If you are motoring around Denmark in the autumn or spring you may have to suffer a more restricted cultural diet, but this should not discourage you from going to Denmark outside the summer season. The scenery and the food and drink are just as good and there is even less traffic on the roads. Also hotels offer cheaper rates while operators like Scandinavian Seaways have some good value motoring packages available.

You will see that I have not included detailed mileages between overnight centres and instead I have given a mileage guide. This is quite deliberate because of the difficulty of determining exact mileages where the smaller roads are involved. Even the Danish kilometre distances on signposts do not always speak the truth! Finally, make sure that you have the right maps with you.

Continued on p.81

Castles and manor houses abound, although very few fall into the fortified and turreted category. They vary in style but usually enjoy very scenic locations. This is one of the buildings that form part of Valdemars Castle which occupies a beautiful location on the island of Tåsinge.

Small cafés and restaurants are plentiful in Denmark offering an enjoyable break from sightseeing. This is Den Lille Cafe in Odense.

ABOVE – The round church at Østerlars on Bornholm which dates back to the 12th century. Round churches are a distinctive feature of the island.

BELOW – Although Denmark has many impressive bridges, ferries still play a very important role. This example links the port of Esbjerg with the delightful island of Fanø.

ABOVE – On the west coast of Jutland are vast sandy beaches backed by sandhills. At Blokhus you can use the beach as a car park or even drive along it to Løkken, the next town.

BELOW – In the heart of the Rebild hills, an attractive area in eastern Jutland, between Hobro and Ålborg.

ABOVE - A placid scene on the Silkeborg lakes as the veteran 1861 paddle steamer Hjejlen makes a call at one of the landing stages.

BELOW - In contrast to Copenhagen and other Danish cities there are many quiet, little places with beautifully kept old houses and cottages. This picturesque street is in Ærøskøbing on the island of Ærø.

77

Ready for the changing of the guard – Danish style. The band lined up in front of the Amalienborg Palace in Copenhagen.

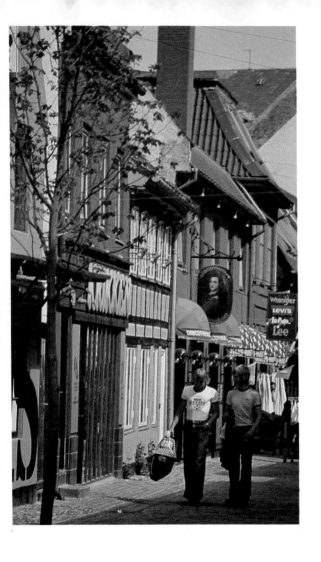

*One of the best known streets in the bustling city of Ålborg is
Jomfru Ane Gade which includes a large number of restaurants of
all kinds. Like many areas in Danish cities and towns it has been
turned into a pedestrian precinct.*

Museums are not all concerned with historical relics or the Viking age, there are others which feature collections ranging from ships in bottles to locomotives. At Ålholm Castle there is a splendid motor museum and also a replica of an early steam train.

SOUTH JUTLAND, FUNEN AND A SPRINKLING OF THE ISLANDS

THIS ITINERARY takes you across Jutland, via Legoland (for those with children) to Vejle, on the attractive Vejle Fjord. Here you should stay two nights to allow for my suggested excursions. You continue south, across the Little Belt bridge to Funen and then take a roundabout route via Bogense to Odense. As there is plenty to see here, a two night stay is recommended. Svendborg, in the south of the island is your next objective, calling at Egeskov Castle en route.

At Svendborg you can make excursions to the islands of Tåsinge and Langeland which are linked by bridges, and to the beautiful island of Ærø, which is reached by ferry.

Your journey continues through the delightful Funen countryside and back on to the peninsula of Jutland to Kolding. You now head south through Christiansfeld, Haderslev (night stop) and Åbenrå to Sønderborg which is a bridge span away on the island of Als. Then it is westward to Tønder, a picturesque little town and, after an overnight stop, on to Møgeltønder (with a little diversion to Rudbøl) and then to the island of Rømø which is linked to Jutland by a long causeway. Ribe is your last night stop, providing an opportunity to see this fascinating little town before motoring to Esbjerg.

Ideally you need 10 nights in Denmark, but this can be reduced to eight if necessary. Alternatively for a shorter stay you can either concentrate on Funen and the islands or, on south Jutland – taking five to seven nights for the former or five nights for the latter.

DAY 1

Leave Esbjerg on the E66 towards Kolding and after about seven miles take the left fork marked to Grindsted (road 30). Bypass the town and follow the signs to Billund (road 28). This large village is the home of Denmark's best known toy – Lego. It is also the home of Denmark's second biggest attraction, Legoland ☆ (**14**). If you have children with you a stop at Legoland is essential; the problem will be getting them away from it. But grown-ups will also find it fascinating with its many different attractions, both indoors and outdoors (it also has good restaurants and a cafeteria). One point to bear in mind is that you have to pay to go on the various rides, but you can buy multi-ride 'Activity Cards' which save money. Adjoining Legoland is the modern Hotel Vis-a-Vis, while nearby is a good camping site. Continue on road 28 to Vejle.

Vejle (**17**) enjoys a notable position at the end of the beautiful Vejle Fjord. Since they built the motorway, which bypasses the town (and crosses the fjord on an immense bridge) the centre has become much improved, especially in summer. Places of interest: Gothic-style Sct. Nicolai Church which has inside it the preserved body of a 2,500-year-old woman found in the

Haraldskær Bog; art museum; and the town's landmark a windmill.

High hills rise on both sides of the town providing good views. Big park on the north side of the fjord, while the road on the south side leads to Munkebjerg (321 ft above sea level), a very beautiful area of woods and walks, in the centre of which is the Munkebjerg Hotel. I consider this to be one of the best hotels in Denmark – for location, comfort and food. It has a splendid position, an excellent restaurant, bar, indoor pool, sauna and solarium and billiards and tennis courts. You can also borrow a bicycle to work off a little weight. Vejle golf course is nearby. Other hotels in Vejle include the Scandic Australia, the modern and comfortable Vejle Center, Park, Dann Inn and Motel Hedegården (nearby). Youth hostel. Camping site.

DAY 2

Suggested excursions from Vejle. Leave the town on the main road north and on the outskirts turn right on road 23, which passes through a mix of scenery to Juelsminde, a minor holiday town. Take the coast road (459) north to Glud, where you bear right to the quiet little fishing hamlet of Snaptun. Minor ferry connecton to Hjarnø. There is a much enlarged and modernised inn, the Snaptun Færgegård. Return to Glud where there is an interesting museum of Danish bygones (**18**). Worth a visit.

Continue along the same road towards Horsens, with the Horsens Fjord in the distance on the right. Beyond the little village of Sejet take a minor road on the left to Bjerre. This takes you through the rather pleasant Bjerre Skov (forest) with attractive walks (plenty of parking places). Follow signs to Sønder (turn right) and then turn left at Nørre Bjerre. This takes you via Stenderup to the main E3 where you turn left and return to Vejle, entering the town on the same road from which you departed.

The second excursion takes you out of Vejle to the north west on the Grejsdalsvej which leads you through the pretty Grejs valley with its densely wooded hillsides and varied landscape. At Sandvad turn left on a minor road which leads you back to road 18. If you have children, turn right to visit the Safari Park ☆ (**16**), near Givskud. Alternatively, turn left to Jelling (**15**) to see the ancient burial mounds and runic stones in the Churchyard. You can also take a veteran steam train from Vejle to Jelling on Sundays in July and early August. From here it is only $7\frac{1}{2}$ miles back to Vejle. Another excursion, without your car, is to take a motor boat trip on the fjord (about $1\frac{1}{2}$ hours, check times with the tourist office).

DAY 3

Leave Vejle on the E67 south. It joins the E66 near the Little Belt which you cross via the imposing suspension bridge. Once

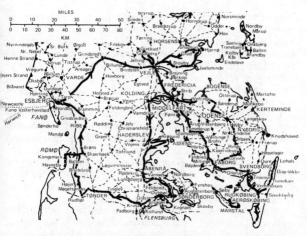

across the bridge, on Funen, take the exit off the motorway and then turn left, crossing over the E66 and follow signs to Bogense. This is something of a quiet backwater, made up of gently rolling farmland. *Bogense* is a little town with a small harbour, a marina and some quiet streets. Hotels: Bogense Hotel, Bogense Kyst Hotel (self-catering holiday hotel). Camping site close to the beach.

Take the Søndersø road (311) and in the village turn right to Morud, turn left and shortly afterwards take a little road to the right which takes you through wooded countryside and past Langesø manor house (not open to the public). You come back to the Morud road (turn left), then to the E66 (join it in the Odense direction). Follow signs into *Odense* (**56**).

DAY 4

With its various places of interest (the principal ones linked with its most famous son, Hans Christian Andersen) it deserves a two night stay. Although an important commercial city and even having a major shipyard you do not really notice the industry. Hotels: H.C. Andersen and Odense Plaza (both large, modern), Windsor (in dull surroundings, but comfortable), Grand (large), City Hotel Odense, Missionshotellet Ansgar, Motel Odense (off-centre, on ring road) and Scandic Hotel Odense (5 miles from city centre). Two camping sites. Youth hostel. Boat trips on the Odense river (see **56** for other attractions).

DAY 5

Leave Odense on road 9 to Kværndrup, then right on road 8, and soon afterwards watch for the right turn to Egeskov Castle ☆

83

(58). A visit to see this fine building and the beautiful park should not be missed. The transport and carriage museums are additional attractions. Return to road 8 and turn right towards Fåborg. This will take you past, on the left, the imposing collection of buildings that make up Brahetrolleborg, the oldest of which was a 15th century abbey. Park open to the public. Restaurant by the park entrance. Just beyond is the village of Korinth (Korinth Kro on the right).

Fåborg has some picturesque features including Vesterport, the town gate (one of the few to be preserved) and the bell tower, the remains of Sct. Nikolaj church, Fåborg museum and Den Gamle Gård museum. Pleasant pedestrian precinct. Leave on road 44 towards Svendborg, but on the outskirts you can fork left on a minor road to Kaleko where there is a restored 600-year-old mill which is now a museum. On the outskirts is the Holiday Hotel Klinten (large, self-catering).

Although it is a modest commercial centre *Svendborg* (59) is also a superb base for the holidaymaker as the southern part of Funen and its off-shore islands are so delightful. It enjoys the almost perfect location by the Sound which is protected by the islands of Thurø and Tåsinge. You really need to spend three nights here, although this could be reduced to two. Hotels: Hotel Svendborg (central, good restaurant, pleasant bedrooms), Ærø, Hotel Royal, Tre Roser (on the outskirts and both a hotel and self-catering centre) and Christiansminde (on the outskirts, a hotel and self-catering centre).

Just outside the town is Christiansminde, a delightful park and beach. Youth hostel which enjoys a nice location. Beyond the park turn right over the causeway on to the horseshoe-shaped little island of *Thurø*. Rather pretty, with two well placed camping sites.

DAYS 6 AND 7

Suggested excursions from Svendborg. One day must be earmarked for a visit to the idyllic island of *Ærø* (61). The ferry takes 75 minutes and on a sunny day there is no better way of passing the time.

Ærøskøbing, where you disembark, is a gem and deserves to be wandered round and savoured. *Marstal*, the old skipper town, is not so pretty-pretty but should also be visited, while the drive from one to the other is very enjoyable. Approaching the town the road runs alongside the beach (mainly shingle) where there are good parking places. There is one main road along the length of the island, running through a series of villages, to another small ferry port, Søby (connections to Fåborg and Mommark).

There is a limited number of hotels on the island, the principal ones being Ærøskøbing - Ærøhus, Det Lille Hotel and

84

Marina (new, with self-catering facilities); Marstal – Danmark, Ærø and Marstal. Camping sites at Ærøskøbing, Marstal and Søby. Youth hostel at Marstal.

For another day out, cross the bridge from Svendborg to the picturesque island of *Tåsinge* (**60**). Follow the signs to *Troense*, which is deservedly called one of the best preserved villages in Denmark. Make a point of seeing the fascinating little maritime museum. Overlooking the Sound, and with splendid views, is the Hotel Troense which has motel-style rooms at the rear. Nearby is Valdemars Castle which enjoys a beautiful setting and includes a museum of interiors. Restaurant in the vaults and a bistro called the Applegarden. As an alternative to driving you can, in mid-summer, sail in the little veteran ship 'Helge' from Svendborg.

If you want to see the island from another viewpoint climb the tower of Bregninge Church. Across the road from the church is a small, but interesting, folklore museum and sea captain's house. At Landet Church you can see the result of a Mayerling-like tragedy. In 1899 Count Sparre killed his lover, the circus artist Elvira Madigan, and then shot himself. Both of them are buried in the churchyard. At Vornæs on the south western side of the island is the Danish Mechanical Dolls Museum (Danmarks Mekaniske Dukkemuseum) ☆ (**60**).

Continue across the island and over the causeway and bridge to the island of *Langeland* (**62**). *Rudkøbing*, the 'capital', is an attractive little town with some well preserved old houses. Museum. Hotel Langeland. Youth hostel. Take the road via Simmerbølle and Tullebølle to *Tranekær* which goes through rolling well-wooded countryside. This pleasant village has, at one end, the impressive red-painted bulk of Tranekær Castle beside the Borresø (lake). There is access to the park. Cafeteria in the former stables or you can refresh yourself at the Tranekær Gjæstgivergaard (inn) near the castle. Lohals at the northern end of the island is a little dull, while at the other end is Bagenkop, a small fishing town which tends to be overrun with holidaymakers from Germany. Nearby is a range of cliffs and a good beach at Ristinge.

If you have time you can also visit, by ferry, the other smaller islands off the coast of Funen, which are *Skarø, Drejø* and *Hjortø*.

DAY 8

Leave Svendborg on road 44 to Fåborg, following the signs to Hårby. Beyond Millinge you will see on the right, the drive leading to Steensgaard Herregårdspension. This impressive three-winged manor house (*c*.1535) is now an hotel and offers a unique atmosphere with its period style bedrooms (but with modern bathrooms) and beautifully furnished sitting rooms and attractive restaurant. The 27-acre park provides peaceful surroundings and it is the sort of place to which I should certainly like to return.

A little further along the road, on the left, is the Falsled Kro which is renowned for its cuisine (and has prices to match its reputation). At Hårby you take the road (329) to Glamsbjerg. Watch for a right turn to Ørsted and go through the village and then follow the sign to Tommerup. On the left is Frøbjerg Bavnehøj, the highest point on Funen (346 ft above sea level). It is an easy climb to the summit where you can enjoy some good views of this part of the island. Return to Ørsted and the main road (turn left) to Assens. Before reaching the latter, turn right on road 313 to Middelfart via Hjorte and Udby. This is an easygoing secondary road that cuts across rural countryside which is now, as in other areas, largely devoted to cereal crops.

On the approach to Middelfart you join the old main road (No. 161) linking Odense with Jutland and which crosses the Little Belt by the first bridge which was completed in 1935. On the approach to the bridge there is a parking area and cafeteria and you can also take a small road on the left which leads down to Hindsgaul, a manor house built in 1785 and now a conference centre and hotel. From here you can walk through the woods to the seashore. You will see a sign to Mindelunden which is a memorial grove dedicated to British aircrew shot down in World War 2. There is a good camping site on this attractive peninsula.

After crossing the Little Belt you keep to the old main road (161) which provides good views of Kolding Fjord on the left. At Taulor, on the right, is the very attractive Kryb-i-Ly inn with some English touches to the furnishings. Follow signs into *Kolding* (**13**) with its massive castle, part of which is a museum. Not the easiest town to drive around, there is a good car park on the left opposite the lake and reasonably close to the castle. Hotels: Saxildhus (by the station), Kolding (near the castle), Hotel Tre Roser and Scanticon-Kolding (hotel and conference centre). Camping sites. Youth hostel.

Depart on the Haderslev road (170), making sure you avoid the E3 motorway. Leave the main road where it is signed to *Christiansfeld* (**6**), the unusual little town established in 1773 by the Moravian Brethren. Two museums: one devoted to the Community of Brethren while the other is the South Jutland Fire Brigade Museum – a strange contrast. The town's speciality (apart from its architecture) is its honey cake.

Continue south on the main road to *Haderslev* (**5**) which has an interesting and historic centre and a spacious park beside the Haderslev Dam (lake). Hotels: Golf Hotel Norden (in the park), Harmonien and Motel Haderslev. Camping site. Youth hostel. This makes a suitable overnight stop or you can go a little further south to Åbenrå.

86

DAY 9

When you leave Haderslev divert on to the road to Osby and Årøsund (small ferry to the island of Årø). Return on the alternative road via Vilstrup, rejoining the main road near Hoptrup. This little excursion is in no way dramatic, just a nice change from motoring down the main road.

Åbenrå is a rather disappointing town; it has some nice old streets, but it has been somewhat overwhelmed by commercial development. At the end of the wide Åbenrå Fjord it should enjoy splendid views but these are spoiled by oil storage tanks on one side and a monumental power station on the other. Interesting museum. Hotel: Hvide Hus (on the outskirts facing the fjord, good rooms). Youth hostel. Numerous camping sites in the area.

Instead of taking the main road to Sønderborg, turn left shortly after passing the power station, and continue through some very enjoyable scenery with occasional views of the Als Fjord. You rejoin the main road a few miles from Sønderborg.

Sønderborg (**3**) on the island of Als, is linked by bridges to Jutland. Impressive castle, busy shopping centre and with attractive surroundings. Hotels: Ansgar, City, Garni and Scandic. Return across the Sound taking the Kruså road (**8**). On the outskirts is Dybbøl Banke (**4**) with its cannon and ramparts associated with the Danish-German war of 1864.

Shortly afterwards take the right fork in the road (481) to *Gråsten,* where the royal summer palace is to be found. The park is open to the public except when the Royal Family is in residence. The palace is now a little overshadowed by industry.

Rejoin the main Kruså road but at Rinkenæs bear left on to the secondary road which runs alongside the Flensborg Fjord. This is a delightful drive through Rønshoved, Sønderhav and Kollund. Several hotels and restaurants along this stretch, plus two well-placed camping sites and a youth hostel.

At the main crossroads at Kruså continue straight ahead (turn left and you are almost immediately at the German frontier) on road 8 and over the motorway. This road takes you through quiet, flat countryside via Rens and Burkal to Tønder.

Tønder (**1**) is worth looking at, with its many preserved houses and an excellent museum. Hotels: Hostrups, Motel Apartments and Abild. Camping site. Youth hostel.

DAY 10

Take the Højer road (419) out of Tønder which brings you to the pretty little village of *Møgeltønder* (**2**). With its cobbled street lined with lime trees and little houses it is very picturesque, while the village church has the oldest working church organ in Denmark (1679). At one end of the village is the Schackenborg Palace and also the Schackenborg Kro.

You can make an intriguing little detour by taking the minor road on the left, beyond Møgeltønder, which is marked to Rudbøl. This is flat, marshland country with an atmosphere of its own. The farms are on raised mounds so that, in the past, they avoided flooding. *Rudbøl* is a most unusual village as the Danish-German border runs down the main street. Danish locals, for example, go shopping at the German supermarket and can be seen wheeling their trolleys back over the border to their cars. Just short of the border is the Rudbøl Grænsekro - an inn dating back to 1791. Behind the old building is a modern complex which is used as a conference centre. There are also some holiday cabins.

The food is to be recommended with several marshland specialities and I had a very satisfying dinner and breakfast when I stayed there. This would make an alternative place to stay to Tønder. From Rudbøl take the Højer road and continue north via Vester Gammelby and then bear left to take the coast road via Koldby and Badsbøl. Then take the left turn (road 175) to the island of *Rømø* (7) which is reached via a six mile long causeway.

When you reach the island, if you drive straight ahead you will come to the magnificent beach which stretches along the west coast. If you turn left this will take you down to the fishing port of Havneby (ferry to Sylt). The north west corner of the island is a restricted military zone. Out of season Rømø is a sleepy place but in high summer it attracts many tourists and is particularly popular with German holidaymakers.

Returning across the causeway, continue to the main road (No. 11) and turn left to Ribe. When you approach the town leave the ring road and follow signs to the centre. *Ribe* (8) is my favourite small town in south Jutland. With its dominant and impressive cathedral in the centre, and the many beautifully preserved houses in the little streets, it has a great deal of charm. It is Denmark's best preserved medieval town and also has some interesting museums (especially Queden's Gård). This should be your last night stop in Denmark and I would recommend the Hotel Dagmar, by the cathedral, which dates back to 1581.

DAY 11

After a morning and perhaps lunch in Ribe there only remains the drive to *Esbjerg* (20 miles). Leave the town on road 11 and then follow the signs to Esbjerg (road 24). There are clear signs to the Englandskajen and your ferry to Britain.

Guide mileages:
Esbjerg - Vejle 54 miles; Vejle - Odense 62 miles; Odense - Svendborg 46 miles; Svendborg - Haderslev 94 miles; Haderslev - Tønder 99 miles; Tønder - Ribe 62 miles; Ribe - Esbjerg 20 miles.

JUTLAND ONLY

ON THIS ITINERARY you go north from Esbjerg, right to the tip of
Jutland, keeping to the west coast, and then returning south
down the eastern side of the peninsula.

Your first day's drive takes you to the pleasant town of
Ringkøbing and after an overnight stay you continue northwards
through typical Jutland scenery via Holstebro and Struer to
Hanstholm.

The following day your route swings eastwards to the city of
Ålborg, with its many attractions. Then it is north west again, to
the area of almost endless beaches and sandhills, passing Denmark's 'little Sahara' and halting at the artists' town of Skagen.

Skagen is the most northerly town on Jutland but you will
want to go the extra two or three miles to the very tip at Grenen.
After an overnight stay, it is time to return southwards, crossing
the Limfjord by ferry and completing the day's drive at Skørping,
near the heart of Denmark's biggest forest.

There are more scenic delights to follow: along minor roads
around the Mariager Fjord and to Mariager itself; then south to
Randers and across the Djursland peninsula to Grenå. The following day is spent exploring the varied attractions of Djursland
before spending your next night at Ebeltoft.

Århus, Denmark's second largest city, is your next destination. Here you should preferably stay two nights before re-
suming your southbound journey again. Your last night is spent
at Vejle before returning to Esbjerg. On this final day you would
have time to reach Ribe for a brief visit or alternatively, if you
have children with you, to stop off at Legoland.

You can complete this itinerary with only nine nights in
Denmark. Ten or eleven nights would be better as this would
provide greater opportunities for local exploration.

DAY 1

Leave Esbjerg on the coast road through Hjerting and then
follow signs to Billum, turning left to Oksbøl (road 431). Here
you take the road that parallels the railway line to Henne Stby.,
where you turn left towards Henne Strand. On the left is Lake
Filsø, a National Trust area, but you turn right through the
Blåbjerg Plantation, a migrating dune 210 ft above sea level. You
join the road (No. 181) from Varde at Nørre Nebel, turning left
towards Nymindegab. Here the road swings north with the sea
on one side and the Ringkøbing Fjord on the other. Between
road and sea are sandhills and meadows dotted with summerhouses and with numerous camping sites. The fjord, on the right,
presents a placid picture with distant views of the opposite shore.
At the south end of the fjord is the attractive Bork Havn Holiday
Centre while at Tipperne there is a bird sanctuary.

Roughly halfway along this road is the fishing harbour of
Hvide Sande while at the end of the fjord, at Søndervig, you turn

right (road 15) to Ringkøbing, six miles to the east.

Ringkøbing (**19**) has a pleasing town centre while the local tourist office has a useful folder which guides you around the little streets with their well-preserved old houses. Hotels: Hotel Fjordgården – modern, well-appointed with comfortable rooms and on the outskirts of town. I have found it a relaxing night stop. In the town: Hotel Ringkøbing (old-established) and Hotel Garni. Youth hostel. For good food try Slippen, a cellar restaurant, while I have also heard good reports about Bøffen.

At Søndervig there is a Danland holiday hotel which is only 200 yards from the wide, sandy beach (reached over the top of the sandhills). Apart from self-catering apartments it also has hotel rooms. A few miles up the coast at Husby Klit is Strandgården, a former farm and an interesting museum of interiors.

DAY 2

Take the Holstebro road (No. 16) and, if you have children, prepare to turn right five miles north at Hee where there is one of the activity parks, Sommerland West (**20**) ☆. Continue on road 16, but bear right at Ulfborg to *Holstebro (***21**), a town which claims to be the cultural centre of western Jutland. It certainly supports the arts and is a good shopping centre. Hotels: Bel Air and Krabbes. Youth hostel.

Continue on road 11 via Struer, a modern town on the Venø Bugt. You leave the town over a causeway and soon reach the Oddesund bridge and enter the area known as Thy (environmentalists note the lines of electricity-producing 'windmills'). A diversion is to take a right turn to Tambohuse where the kro (inn) makes a pleasant stop for lunch. The countryside now becomes more varied and at Hurup you take a left turn on to road 545 marked to Vestervig where there is the largest village church in Scandinavia.

This secondary road goes through pleasant scenery and at Vestervig look for the left turn, in the main street, to Krik and Agger (not very clearly signed). The *Agger Tange* is a long spit of land, with water on both sides, which ends at the ferry for Thyborøn. This is a very good area for bird watching (web-footed and wading birds) and also for sea fishing. There are two modern and well-equipped self-catering holiday centres in this area: the Hotel Agger Tange and the Feriehotel Krik Vig.

Look for the minor road which takes you past Ørum Sø (lake) and Tolbøl and Ørum. Immediately after the latter village turn right and shortly afterwards turn left on the secondary road from Vestervig to Klitmøller (No. 181). To the right you will see in the distance the Morup Mølle Kro which might be worth a slight detour for refreshments or a meal. There is excellent fishing at this Kro and the Hvidbjerg river actually runs through the inn's garden.

Continue along the secondary road to *Klitmøller* which wends its way through a nice mix of fields, woods and heathland, interspersed with small lakes and streams. A considerable amount of land in this area belongs to the Danish National Trust. Another little detour involves a left turn to Nørre Vorupør, one of the last fishing hamlets on the west coast where the boats are hauled up on to the beach. It also has an aquarium. Klitmøller, where you reach the coast, is a former fishing harbour and now a holiday village with summerhouses.

The next stretch of the road to Hantsholm runs through wild and quite spectacular scenery with the beach and sandhills on the left and the Hansted Reservat on the right. This was formerly rolling dunes which have now become a treeless heathland. It is an area rich in bird and wild life. There are no roads across it and it is closed to the public during the breeding season (April 15 – July 16).

Hantsholm, like the scenery around it, is unusual. In 1917 the Danish Government decided to build a harbour here but the work only proceeded very slowly. In World War 2 the occupying German forces made it a major fortified zone so that, with a similar fortified area in Norway, the entrance to the Baltic was controlled.

In the 1960's the construction of a new harbour and town was begun. The town plan allowed commercial, residential and shopping areas to be segregated with heath and woodland between them. The town is therefore spread out over a wide area and the harbour cannot be seen as it lies at the base of steep chalk cliffs.

There are two museums, one by the lighhouse and the other in one of the former gun emplacements. There is a good viewpoint on the cliffs, which overlooks the harbour and the sea (restaurant nearby). Hotel: Hotel Hantsholm, modern and well-appointed with a good restaurant, welcoming atmosphere. On the minor road to Vigsø there is a well-located camping site.

DAY 3

The Thisted road (No. 26) is your exit from Hantsholm, but take the left fork (road 29) to Østerild and Fjerritslev. Just short of Østerild take the left turn to Bjerget and Vust which is an alternative route to Fjerritslev. This begins as a pretty tree-lined road and later the scenery becomes much more rolling. At Bjerget you can enjoy a splendid view across the Lund Fjord (there is a useful lay-by on the left) while in the other direction there is a vista of heathlands as far as the eye can see.

A short and worthwhile detour is to take the left turn at the end of the Lund Fjord to Bulbjerg. This is a piece of limestone 130 ft high from which you have outstanding views of the area which is known as the 'shoulder of Denmark'.

At Fjerritslev (**48**) turn right to Aggersund (road 29). You will cross the Aggersund by a bridge and a few miles beyond there is a left turn to Brøndum and Nibe. This road goes through gentle, rural countryside and at a T-junction you will see that Nibe is signed in both directions. Take the left-hand road which is the longer and more picturesque route via Kølby and Farstrup which brings you down by the water at Sebbersund. The road follows the curve of the bay beyond which is *Nibe* (**45**), a quiet little town of narrow streets and cottages and with a small harbour.

Continue through the town on the road (No. 187) to Ålborg, Denmark's fourth largest city which lies on the Limfjord. Although it is a major industrial and commercial centre (among the products made here is aquavit) it remains an interesting and lively city, offering plenty to do and see (check entry **44** in the 'Attractions for Children and Adults' chapter). Hotels: Hvide Hus (few minutes from the city centre), the restaurant, 16 floors up, offers panoramic views. Rooms are well-equipped. Others: Hotel Phønix, first-class, old-established and nearer the city centre. Limfjordshotellet (close to restaurants, shops) and Slotshotellet, both modern with well-appointed rooms. Central Hotel, Park Hotel, Hotel Hafnia, Hotel Ansgar and, on the outskirts, the Scandic Hotel and Hotel Scheelsminde. Youth hostel. There is a marvellous choice of restaurants plus several nightclubs and discos and for a drink with atmosphere try Duus Vinkjælder in Jens Bangs Stenhus. A two night stay would provide more time to explore the city and be worthwhile.

DAY 4

Cross the bridge spanning the Limfjord to Nørresundby and turn left (roads 11/55). At Åbybro bear right on road 55. Beyond Panderup there is a left turn to *Blokhus*, a village of 200 inhabitants which has now grown into a major Danish holiday centre. There is a large Danland self-catering hotel, the Nordsøen, which is a dominant feature. Youth hostel. The wide, firm, sandy beach is backed by sandhills and simply stretches away into the distance.

You can drive all the way along the beach to *Løkken* (**49**) about 10 miles away – but watch out for bathers and observe the speed limits. On the way to Blokhus you will see a sign on the left which points to Fårup Sommerland (**50**) ☆, the pioneer among the activity parks which now has a giant Aquapark.

If you don't take to the beach, return to road 55 and motor on to Løkken. On the way, there is a left turn to *Grønhøj*, an area of summerhouses plus a major self-catering hotel, the Grønhøj Strand. Løkken is another, and even larger, seaside resort with many summerhouses, several hotels, a self-catering centre and no less than 11 camping sites, plus numerous restaurants. Quite appealing if the weather is good and if you like seaside resorts.

Returning to the main road turn left and shortly afterwards take a right turn to Børglum. On top of high ground is a traditional windmill and nearby the impressive white-washed bulk of the Børglum Monastery (**51**). From here take the minor road to Vittrup and as you leave the monastery you will have a superb view of this entire area of Jutland.

At the main road at Vittrup turn right and then left at Sønder Rubjerg to Lønstrup. You will now see the huge sandhills at *Rubjerg Knude* (**52**) and if the wind is blowing (as it usually is along this coast) it will whip the sand up in an amazing fashion. Turn left down the narrow road to Rubjerg lighthouse, which is now almost hidden behind the sandhills. There is an interesting museum in the lighthouse and in an adjoining building there is a cafeteria where you get sand with everything. A highly unusual location and well worth seeing, though you will be feeling a bit sandy after your visit.

Rejoin the road to Lønstrup and continue to *Hjørring,* the ancient capital of Vendsyssel, the name given to this particular region of Jutland. It is now a modern commercial town but it retains an attractive older part which is worth a few minutes' inspection. There is an interesting historical museum of Vendsyssel in the town. Leave on road 13 to Hirtshals and bear right on the secondary road via Bjergby, Uggerby and Tversted (on road 597). As you approach the main road (No. 40) to Skagen you will see the outline of *Råbjerg Mile* (**54**) on your left. This is a remarkable sand desert surrounded by heathland. It is best approached on the Kandestederne road which is a left turn at Hulsig off the main road to Skagen.

As you approach Skagen you will be able to see the sea on both sides of the now very narrow peninsula. *Skagen* (**55**) is somewhat uninspiring to begin with, but keep going and it will improve and become much more picturesque. It has quite a large fishing harbour and the older parts of the town are very attractive and full of charm. It is one of Denmark's oldest and most distinctive resorts as well as being the 'artists town' (because of the unusual quality of the light reflected from the sea on three sides). Hotels: Brøndums (old-established and reputedly very good), Hotel Skagen (modern, on the outskirts), Hotel Inger. Youth hostel. Four camping sites in the area.

You can drive three miles beyond the town to Grenen at the very tip of Jutland. From here you can walk across the sandhills to where the waters of the Kattegat and Skagerrak meet. By the car park is a restaurant and cafeteria and an art gallery.

DAY 5

Return south on road No. 40 to *Frederikshavn* (**53**). Busy ferry port with connections to Norway and Sweden and the little island of Læsø. The Bangsbo museum is particularly fascinating and should be seen, while the Krudttårnsmuseet is also of interest. Splendid views from the 196 ft high Cloostårnet tower. Hotels: Frederikshavn (modern, with a super tropical wonderland pool in the centre), Jutlandia (modern, extensively refurbished, excellent), Hoffmanns, Park, Mariehønen, Turisthotellet, Motel Lisboa.

Keep on the E3 to Hjallerup where you turn left to Dronninglund. This road takes you past the Dronninglund Castle which is now a most attractive hotel and conference centre (quiet, not really suitable for children, open 11 June – 14 Aug). Continue to Aså where you turn right along a road which parallels the coast, although it is often screened by woods. This is another summerhouse area, while at Hou there are two well-placed camping sites. Drive down to the little ferry berth at Hals for the six-minute crossing to Egense. This road also keeps to the coast and at Dokkedal bear right on the road through Kongenslev and Lyngby to Skørping.

Skørping is a small town on the edge of Denmark's largest forest – the Rold Skov (15,800 acres) and close to the Rebild Hills (**41**). Hotels: Rebild Park, in the centre of Skørping, close to the railway but having excellent rooms and a good restaurant with a pleasant atmosphere. Youth hostel. Not far away in the heart of the forest, is the Rold Stor Kro, built in 1958. There are fine views of the Rebild hills from the restaurant and it has a large comfortable lounge, an indoor pool and bar, sauna, exercise room and solarium. Several camping sites in the area. There are some lovely walks in the Rebild hills.

DAY 6

At the main E3 turn left to Hobro, but just before this town is reached take the left turn to Hadsund (road 541). At Valsgård take a sharp right turn in the village. This road is quite elevated and affords some good views of the surrounding countryside. Watch for a right turn to Krogen, which is a minor road, you then bear right again on to an even smaller road which soon becomes an unsurfaced track. Here you look down over the Mariager Fjord.

The track – which is quite negotiable – twists and turns through the woods and eventually passes a solitary farm and crosses a small dam. On the left is the small Kielstrup lake and on the right the fjord. At the end of the dam take the right hand track. This is a remote and quite enchanting area and worthy of exploration. The track leads you down into the tiny little village of Stinesminde with its small harbour (notice the eel traps). Take the same road out of the village but turn right at a T-junction which leads you to the Hobro – Hadsund road again at Our.

At Hadsund turn right over the bridge and then right again on the road to Assens and Mariager (No. 556) – an attractive drive to an appealing little town. *Mariager* – the town of roses – with its cobbled streets and sleepy air is a good place to break your journey for a while. Abbey and museum. Preserved railway **(40)** ☆. Hotel: Postgården – charming with good food.

Leave the town on the Randers road, along which at the little village of Hvidsten is the pretty, half-timbered Hvidsten Kro, in my opinion one of the most attractive inns on Jutland. The little rooms are stuffed with interesting bygones while the culinary speciality is a bacon omelette served in the pan. But there is another aspect to the Hvidsten Kro: in World War 2 it was one of the centres of the Danish resistance movement and the owner of the inn and a number of the villagers were discovered and subsequently shot. Their memorial is in the churchyard.

Randers, a busy commercial and industrial town, is also a good shopping centre. There are some preserved old buildings and a number of the principal streets have been pedestrianised. It is not the easiest town to negotiate by car and if you decide to stop it is best to find a car park and explore on foot. Hotels: Randers (in the centre), Scandic Kongens Ege (modern, elevated position and just outside the centre). Leave Randers on road 16 to Grenå.

Grenå **(35)** is a small town and ferry port (connections to Zealand, Sweden and the little island of Anholt). Hotels: Du Nord – modern single storey building (only the restaurant is upstairs) with well-appointed rooms, outdoor pool, lounge and bar. At nearby Gjerrild there is the Gjerrild Kro and Motel. Two camping sites in Grenå and several others in the area. Youth hostel at Gjerrild.

DAY 7

This day involves only a short drive to your next night stop at Ebeltoft. Alternatively you could spend two nights at Grenå or, instead, two nights at Ebeltoft. Your free time will give you an opportunity to explore the attractive Djursland peninsula. Children will probably opt for Djurs Sommerland **(36)** ☆, a super activity park off the Grenå – Randers road (from Grenå take the third left turn to Nimtofte which is signed). For railway enthusiasts there is the little museum at Ryomgård **(37)** ☆. Other places of interest include Gammel Estrup Castle **(38)** at Auning; Clausholm Castle **(39)** at Voldum; Sostrup Castle (now a convent, retreat and guest house) near Gjerrild; Meilgård Castle (not open, but in beautiful surroundings and with part of the stables converted to a restaurant); and Rosenholm Castle, near Hornslet.

There are good beaches with safe bathing south of Grenå and at Bønnerup near Gjerrild, to the north. There are numerous other castles and manor houses which are not open to the public (but which can usually be seen from a public road) such as

Katholm, Rugård, Løvenholm and Skaføgård. Also runic stones at Rimsø, where there is Denmark's oldest vicarage (*c.*1593) and, near Tåstrup, a prehistoric burial site with dolmens and a passage grave.

Study the local brochures and the map and then decide on where you want to go. Ebeltoft, your overnight destination, can be reached from various directions – the shortest way from Grenå is on road 15, bearing left at Tirstrup and then following the signs.

DAY 8

One of Denmark's oldest towns, *Ebeltoft* (**34**), is now in the centre of a popular holiday area. It is on the attractive Ebeltoft Bay while the Mols country to the west, with its hummocky hills, is quite appealing. Hotels: Ebeltoft Strand (modern, by the beach); Hvide Hus (large, overlooks the bay from an elevated position); Ebeltoft Park Hotel (new, on the outskirts); Hotel Vægtergården (at Femmøller Strand to the west of Ebeltoft); Hotel Vigen (in the centre). Youth hostel. There are eight camping sites in the area and nearby is the Øer maritime holiday centre, an imaginative arrangement of self-catering 'villages' on seven small artificial islands.

Leave Ebeltoft on the road to Rønde, via Femmøller and Egens which takes you past the ruins of Kalø Castle (on the left and at the end of a little causeway). At Rønde you join road 15 to Århus.

In spite of being a major industrial and commercial centre and having a busy harbour, *Århus* (**28**) is a very enjoyable city with a host of attractions and excellent shops – see the chapter on 'Attractions for Children and Adults'. Hotels: Marselis – lovely position by the Marselisborg Forest and facing the bay; Hotel Kong Christian d.X, very modern and more a business hotel with an excellent restaurant. Other hotels: Hotel Atlantic (large, central), Hotel Ritz (very central, by the station), Mission Hotel Ansgar (also by the station), Hotel Windsor, Park Hotel, Eriksens Hotel and Hotel Royal (a central old-established hotel, now refurbished). Several camping sites. Youth hostel. There is a wide range of restaurants plus several nightclubs and discothèques. Because of its choice of attractions Århus really deserves a two-night stay.

DAY 9

Motor south from Århus on the Odder road, taking a left turn marked to Moesgård, where the Museum of Pre-History is in a former manor house. After visiting the museum (if you have the time) follow the minor road to Ajstrup and Norsminde where you cross the Norsminde Fjord by a short causeway. Here there is an attractive inn, the Norsminde Gammel Kro (which dates

97

back to 1693), speciality fried eels.

Carry on through Saksild and Odder where you follow the signs to Skanderborg (road 445). Here you should take the old main road (No. 170) south rather than the E3 motorway, although both come together near Horsens. Continue south to *Vejle* (**17**) at the head of the Vejle Fjord. Hotels: Scandic Australia, Vejle Center (modern, good value, welcoming), Park, Vejle, Motel Hedegården and the Munkebjerg, three miles along the southern shore of the fjord. It enjoys a splendid elevated position, surrounded by woods and maintains a high standard of comfort and cuisine. A good choice for your last night in Denmark.

DAY 10

Take the Kolding road out of Vejle but bear right before leaving the town on the 'Ribevej' signed to Esbjerg (No. 417). However if you have children you should leave Vejle on road 28 to Billund and *Legoland* (**14**) ☆. It is 36 miles from Legoland to Esbjerg so allow yourself sufficient time to drive to the ferry - even if you have to extricate your offspring by force.

The alternative is to continue along the secondary road to the E66. Here you can turn right for Esbjerg, but if you have two or three hours in hand, cross the main road and continue south via Foldingbro on road 32 to *Ribe* (**8**). Go into the town centre with its imposing cathedral and well preserved townscape. Ribe is 20 miles from Esbjerg so allow time for your journey to the port.

The approach to the ferry terminal is well signed whether you are coming from Billund or Ribe.

Guide mileages:
Esbjerg - Ringkøbing 62 miles; Ringkøbing - Hantsholm 103 miles;
Hantsholm - Ålborg 70 miles; Ålborg - Skagen 97 miles;
Skagen - Skørping 103 miles; Skørping - Grenå 91 miles;
Grenå - Ebeltoft 22 miles; Ebeltoft - Århus 31 miles;
Århus - Vejle 61 miles; Vejle - Esbjerg (via Legoland) 54 miles;
Vejle - Esbjerg (via Ribe) 75 miles; Vejle - Esbjerg (direct) 58 miles.

MAINLY CENTRAL JUTLAND

CENTRAL JUTLAND includes some of Denmark's finest scenery and this itinerary not only takes you to the heart of it, but also encompasses the cities of Ålborg and Århus and the Djursland peninsula.

An indirect route from Esbjerg to Vejle occupies the first day and after an overnight stop you pursue a meandering route to and through Denmark's beautiful lake district. This is one of the most appealing areas of the country with its enjoyable mix of lakes, hills and forests.

Silkeborg is in the centre of the region; naturally that is where you pause before following another irregular course so you can see various places of interest. Your destination is Skive, and the next morning there is an opportunity to visit the fascinating open air museum at Hjerl Hede and also Spøttrup Castle. Then you take a north-easterly route across Salling and Himmerland to the busy city of Ålborg on the Limfjord.

There is time to see something of the city before heading south because your day's motoring is quite brief – to Skørping, on the edge of Denmark's largest forest, the Rold Skov. After an overnight stay you continue southwards through the pretty little town of Mariager and an unspoilt area to the south-east which is well off the tourist track. Your day's journey is completed with a drive through some of the Djursland peninsula's most delightful scenery, before reaching Grenå.

Most of the next day is available for you to explore this region with its good beaches, gently rolling countryside and numerous castles and manor houses. You stay at Ebeltoft, a picturesque little town overlooking an equally attractive bay.

Århus, where you spend your last night in Denmark, is the country's second largest city and provides plenty of opportunities to fill your time, in fact two nights here would be preferable.

Your final day follows the most direct motorway route to Esbjerg and there is ample time to reach the port before your ferry departs for England.

This itinerary involves a minimum of eight nights in Denmark but you would certainly be able to see more by extending your stay to nine or 10 nights. An extra night at Silkeborg and Århus would be my recommendation.

DAY 1

The main Kolding/Odense road, the E66, is your exit from Esbjerg. Roughly halfway to Kolding, at Holsted, you leave the main road and turn left on to the 425. When you approach Hovborg turn right into the village and then in the centre turn right on to the minor road to Vorbasse.

Just before you turn you will see on the left the attractive 150-year-old Hovborg Kro, a famous moorland inn and now considerably extended. The Vorbasse road takes you through a forested area which is comparatively flat. At Vorbasse bear left and then right on the road to Skjoldbjerg and Store Almstok. This takes you round the edge of Randbøl Heath, which can be seen in the distance to the right.

When you reach the secondary road (No. 176) from Egtved to Billund you turn left. As you approach Billund, turn right on to road 28 to Vejle. If, on the other hand, you have children, they will demand that you go straight on and follow the signs to Legoland (**14**) ☆.

Vejle (**17**), at the end of the fjord, enjoys a splendid position with hills (and comparatively high ones for Denmark) on either side of it while to the north-west is the appealing landscape of the Grejs valley. The heavy traffic that used to come through the centre now uses the motorway that bypasses the town and crosses the fjord on a magnificent bridge. Both the north and south sides of the fjord are very beautiful. There is a big wooded area on the former, while on the southern shore the road eventually climbs steeply to Munkebjerg, 320 ft above sea level. Among the woods is the Munkebjerg Hotel, renowned for its comfort and cuisine and a great favourite of mine. At the hotel you can go for walks, borrow a bicycle, play tennis or go for a swim. Other hotels in Vejle are the Scandic Australia, Vejle Center (modern, cheerful), Park, Vejle and Motel Hedegården. Youth hostel.

DAY 2

Take the Herning road (No. 18) and pause at Jelling (**15**) to see the two huge burial mounds and the runic stones in the church-yard. One of the stones depicts the crucifixion and because it tells of the introduction of Christianity to Denmark it is often called Denmark's birth certificate. Continue to Givskud where there is a large safari park (**16**) ☆ where you can drive for five miles among the animals: camels, llamas, elephants and up to 40 lions. Here you turn right on to a minor road through Nørre Kolle-morten to road 13, where you turn left to Nørre Snede, this road taking you through a wooded area. In Nørre Snede take the right fork to Bryrup and Silkeborg (road 453).

On the way to Bryrup the scenery is not very interesting, but at the end of the village turn left to Vrads when there is a marked change as this little road winds up and down through hills and woodland. Just short of Vrads, on the left, is the end of the Bryrup-Vrads preserved railway (**23**) ☆. The station build-ing is now a small restaurant. In Vrads village look for the sign to Asklev and take this minor road which crosses Vrads Sande, an extensive moorland area. Originally it was fertile ground but it was destroyed by drifting sand in the 17th century. Nearby is Vrads Sande Holiday Centre.

Right turn at Asklev on to the road to Them, which con-tinues through pleasant country before you turn left to

Rodelund. There is a staggered crossroads at Rodelund and you need to make a right and a left turn in order to gain road 445 to Ry and Himmelbjerget. It is along this road that you turn left to get to one of Denmark's most scenic viewpoints: Himmelbjerget or 'heavenly mountain'.

There are plenty of walks in the area but the most popular one brings you to the tower, built in 1875, on the summit. From this point there are magnificent views over the lakes and surrounding countryside.

Return to the Ry road and when you reach this little town

take a left turn immediately beyond the railway crossing followed by another left turn signed to Laven. This road through Laven to Silkeborg is most attractive with views of the lake on the left and the distant hills beyond. At Laven you can turn down by the lake for a short pause to take in the scenery. A little further on is the Terrassen Restaurant, on the right, which has a splendid outlook. There are several good camping sites in the immediate area.

In *Silkeborg* (**24**) turn left to reach the town centre. The heart of the town is pedestrianised but there are plenty of peripheral car parks. Don't forget to visit the museum and see the head of the 2,200-year-old 'Tollund Man' – slightly macabre but fascinating. You can also take trips on the lake on the splendid little paddle steamer 'Hjejlen', built in 1861 and still going strong. Hotels: Dania (central), and Impala (modern, just outside the town centre on road 15 with a nice position overlooking the lake. Good, but quite expensive, restaurant).

DAY 3

Leave on the road passing the Langsø (lake) on the left but instead of joining the main Herning – Århus road (No. 15) continue straight on, through Voel. At Skannerup turn left to Gjern and on reaching this village turn right to the Jutland Car Museum (**25**) ☆. Now, you may not be particularly interested in old motor cars but this museum is worth a visit just to see the quality of the exhibits. The museum is virtually the work of one man and his family and the restoration of three or four cars is completed each year.

Head now for the Århus – Viborg road (No. 26) and turn left. This takes you past the Tange lake (good lay-by on the right, camping site and youth hostel on the left) and through Rødkærsbro to *Viborg* (**27**) a town on a hill which dips down to two small lakes, the Nørresø and Søndersø. If you want a break there is a park by the Nørresø.

Leave town on road 16 towards Holstebro and after about eight miles turn right to Mønsted where you will find the Mønsted Limestone Mines (Kalk Gruber) **26** ☆. You can go down into the disused mine workings, parts of which are now used to mature tons of cheese. Limestone was first extracted from this area in the 10th century and, among other things, was used in the building of Ribe Cathedral.

Return to the main road and when you reach Sjørup turn right to *Skive* (road 186). The town has no particular attractions but it makes a useful overnight stop. Hotels: Gl. Skivehus (old established, on a busy crossroads and by the river. Some bedrooms rather disappointing, but the food in the restaurant is excellent and the service brisk and cheerful). Hilltop (modern, just outside the town centre, elevated position, good food).

102

DAY 4

Your route begins on road 189 to Hvidbjerg but before you have
cleared the town turn left on the 34 to Estvad. Keep to this road
until you see the sign on the right to Hjerl Hede and Sevel. Hjerl
Hede (29) ☆ is a remarkable and extensive open air museum
with over 40 authentic buildings, plus a stone age settlement, on
a 40 acre site. They give a good impression of how people lived
and worked in the past. There is a forestry museum and you can
also see how peat was extracted and processed.

The museum covers only a fragment of the 2,500 acres of
National Trust land that makes up Hjerl Hede, considered to be
one of Denmark's most impressive untouched natural areas and
which is bisected by a large lake, the Flyndersø.

On leaving the museum follow the signs to Sahl and Ål
where you bear right to Ejsing, crossing the road from Vinderup.
Beyond Ejsing head for Geddal, turn right, then left to Lem and
Lihme and on to Ålbæk. It may sound a little complicated, but it
is worth it. This is an appealing, unspoilt area with the waters of
the Venø Bugt on your left. You are making for Spøttrup Castle
which is, from this direction, rather badly signed (I have to admit
I went astray). Basically you have to bear right and right again.
The double-moated castle (30) c.1500 also has a small renaissance garden with medieval herbs and medicinal plants.

Follow the road beyond the castle and then turn left to
Rødding and right to Krejbjerg and continue on this minor road
until you reach a T-junction. Turn left and when road 26 is
reached shortly afterwards turn right but almost immediately
take the minor road on the left to Roslev (very pleasant inn – the
Roslev Kro – good for refreshments or lunch). At Kirkeby turn
right and follow the signs to Sundsøre. If you have time you
should continue north from Kirkeby to Branden and take the
ferry to the little island of Fur (five minute crossing). This has
steep moler clay cliffs and also an interesting museum.

Returning to the original route, at Sundsøre you take the
ferry to Hvalpsund (crossing time 12 minutes). On leaving the
ferry the road climbs quite sharply from the little harbour and the
countryside also undergoes a change being softer and more
varied. If you want you can turn right at Hvalpsund to Hessel
where there is the last fully thatched manor house. Most of the
buildings are 300 years old and now form part of an interesting
museum of interiors and agriculture. Your route is through the
Himmerland area via Farsø and Hornum on road 187, crossing
the 29, and on through Bislev to Nibe (45), a picturesque small
town on the Limfjord. Have a look at its narrow little streets and
pretty cottages before continuing to Ålborg.

Ålborg has always had the reputation for being a lively city
(44) and it does offer the visitor a variety of attractions and

entertainment (see the entry in the chapter on 'Attractions for Children and Adults'). One thing which is enjoyable is a stroll through the old parts of the city and the tourist office has a useful little folder – 'Good Old Ålborg' – which takes you on a guided tour. Hotels: Hvide Hus, just out of the centre, in a park; Phønix, old-established, first class; Limfjordshotellet and Slotshotellet, both modern and central. Also Central Hotel, Park Hotel, Hotel Hafnia and Scandic (on the outskirts), Ansgar. Youth hostel.

DAY 5

As your journey is comparatively short, you could spend the morning in Ålborg before leaving. You turn on to road 595 to Klarup but on the fringe of the city turn right on to road 507 to Hadsund. Beyond Fjellerad bear right and follow the signs to Skørping. Nothing of exceptional note along this road but it is preferable to taking the main E3.

Skørping is on the edge of the Rold Skov forest and close to the Rebild Hills (**41**). Make a point of going to the latter which offer some splendid views and are quite a surprise in a country which is supposed to be nearly flat. Two other short excursions you can take are to Thingbæk Kalkminer and to Store Blåkilde. The former is an old limestone mine, close to the main E3, and in the galleries are more than 100 sculptures by two famous Danish artists, Bundgård and Bonnesen. Store Blåkilde (the Big Blue Spring) is off the Skørping – Astrup road and is a crater from which a reputed seven million gallons of water bubble up every 24 hours. The Rebild Park hotel has comfortable rooms, and a good restaurant (but is close to the railway). A few miles away, in the forest, is the Rold Stor Kro, which is a very attractive resort hotel. There are fine views from the restaurant and there is a comfortable lounge and an indoor pool. Youth hostel and camping site near Skørping.

DAY 6

Make for the E3, turn left towards Hobro. Descend into the town and on leaving turn left on the road to *Mariager* (No. 555). Often called the town of roses, Mariager is a quiet little place with its cobbled streets. Down by the harbour is the terminus of the Mariager – Handest Veteran Railway (**40**) ☆, another of Denmark's preserved railways.

Continue on the road to Assens which affords some very good views across the Mariager Fjord. Just beyond Assens bear right on the minor road through Falslev and Norup to the Hadsund – Randers road (No. 507) where you turn right. About three miles along this road turn left to Havndal where you bear left to Klattrup. At the latter you again keep left and follow this meandering little road past Overgård, an attractive manor house which is well-screened by trees (not open to the public). This road now doubles back to the village of Udbyneder. You get some nice views along this road which is a tranquil out of the way area but having a distinct appeal of its own.

From Udbyneder follow the sign to Dalbyneder where you turn left and at a minor crossroads turn left again, this road being marked to Udbyhøj. Here you take the ferry across the mouth of the Randers Fjord (crossing time five minutes).

It is equally quiet on the south side of the fjord and when you reach Udby, take a left turn to Ingerslev where you are now much closer to the sea. You pass Estrupland manor house with its big adjoining farm buildings and continue via Store Sjørup and Hevring. A few miles beyond the last named village you reach the Allingåbro – Grenå road (No. 547) near Vivild and turn left.

This road takes you through rolling farmland and wooded areas and there are several camping sites to the left of the road which must be quite close to the coast. Watch for the sign on the left to Meilgård and Bønnerup Strand. This is a pretty little road which leads you to the white-washed Meilgård Castle. Although not open to the public, you can walk in the grounds. There is a restaurant in the former stables.

Bønnerup Strand is a seaside village with a good beach and safe bathing (suitable for children). At the small harbour is a boat for hire which will take you out for some good fishing or you can try your luck from the shore. There is a self-catering holiday centre here. Follow the signs to Gjerrild, a pretty little village with its limestone church dating back to the 12th century. The interior has some beautiful frescoes. Gjerrild Kro and Motel and a youth hostel. Nearby is Sostrup Castle which is now a convent, retreat and guest house and is worth looking at.

Follow the signs into *Grenå*, a small town and ferry port (connections to Zealand, Sweden and the little island of Anholt). Good beaches to the south of the town. Hotels: Du Nord. Two camping sites in Grenå. This itinerary is based on staying one night here and one night in Ebeltoft but you can just as well stay two nights at either of these centres.

DAY 7

This day gives you an opportunity to see something of the Djurs area. There are several interesting castles, manor houses and museums such as Gammel Estrup Castle (**38**), Clausholm Castle (**39**) and Rosenholm Castle. For children there is the marvellous Djurs Sommerland (**36**) ☆ which I thought was extremely well run and entertaining. Get some of the local brochures from the tourist offices in Grenå or Ebeltoft – you will find plenty to occupy your time.

Ebeltoft (**34**) is an attractive small town which still retains some cobbled streets and enjoys a beautiful location on a semicircular bay. There is also a ferry connection from here to Zealand. Hotels: Ebeltoft Strand (modern, by the sea); Hvide Hus (enjoying an elevated position); Ebeltoft Park Hotel (on the outskirts, looks very pleasant); Hotel Vigen (in the town centre). At Femmøller Strand to the west of Ebeltoft is the Hotel Vægtergården and to the east is the new Øer maritime holiday centre on seven little artificial islands. Youth hostel. Numerous camping sites.

DAY 8

Your destination is Århus and you can either take the road to Rønde via Femmøller and Egens or make a detour through the attractive hilly Mols area, via Fuglsø, Torup, Knebel and Vrinners. Whichever route you opt for, you will pass the ruins of Kalø Castle on your left before reaching Rønde and joining the main road (No. 15) to Århus.

The chapter on 'Attractions for Children and Adults' has a useful entry for *Århus* (**28**) and gives you a good idea of what the city has to offer (although even this is not exhaustive, but just highlights some of the more interesting things). This is why the city really does deserve a two night stay if you have the time. Hotels: Marselis (de luxe and enjoying a superb position on the city's outskirts by the Marselisborg Forest), Kong Christian d.X (de luxe, modern, splendid food), Atlantic (big, in the centre), Ritz (central, comfortable), Mission Hotel Ansgar (central), Windsor, Park, Eriksens and Royal (central, expensive). Youth hostel.

DAY 9

A journey direct to Esbjerg keeping at first to the southbound E3 motorway via Horsens and Vejle (using the bypass over that splendid bridge). At the intersection of the E3 and the E66 follow the signs for Esbjerg.

Guide mileages:
Esbjerg - Vejle 58 miles; Vejle - Silkeborg 63 miles;
Silkeborg - Skive 56 miles; Skive - Ålborg 79 miles;
Ålborg - Skørping 22 miles; Skørping - Grenå 84 miles;
Grenå - Ebeltoft 22 miles; Ebeltoft - Århus 31 miles;
Århus - Esbjerg 105 miles.

LOITERING WITH INTENT

MOST OF THE itineraries in this book are based on the assumption that you want to see as much as you possibly can of a particular area of Denmark. Time is allowed for seeing places of interest but usually your stays are limited to just one night at each town. But this itinerary is something of an exception as it includes longer stops which afford greater opportunities for local sight-seeing or plain idleness. I also suggest specific hotels which have been selected both for their location and their quality.

You start by motoring across Jutland and through the island of Funen to an hotel which is in a former manor house. Here you can make a variety of excursions before moving on across the islands of Tåsinge and Langeland and on to the island of Lolland. Your base is the small town of Maribo which is rough-ly in the centre of the island.

From Lolland you continue across Falster and on to the island of Zealand to a particularly pleasant inn near the town of Næstved. This makes a good base from which to explore this region or you could even make a day trip to Copenhagen.

You return to Jutland via an alternative route to, and through Funen. Your last stop is at Munkebjerg, a short distance from Vejle. Finally you motor south-westwards for a brief visit to the beautiful little town of Ribe before departing from Esbjerg for England.

The minimum stay at each centre is two nights, making eight nights in all, but it would be much better to increase the total to 10 nights. The extra nights would be spent in those areas which appeal to you most.

TO FUNEN

Going east across Jutland on the E66 from Esbjerg is not the best introduction to Denmark for the first time visitor. While it is cer-tainly not unpleasant, it is also not very inspiring, but at least you are getting this stretch over first. Beyond Kolding you should leave the motorway (as the E66 has now become) and drop down on to the old main road (No. 161) passing, at Taulov, the very pleasant (if unpronounceable) Kryb-i-ly Kro (inn). This will take you nearer Kolding Fjord and across to the island of Funen on the old combined rail and road bridge.

Shortly after leaving the bridge there is a wooded area with car parks. Turn right down a small road leading to Hindsgaul, a manor house with a neo-classical main building of the 'Funen School' built in 1785. It is now a conference centre and private hotel. From the adjoining car park you can walk down to the shore on Fænø Sund or through the park to cliffs to the west. You can take a longer walk round the tip of the peninsula, following an arrowed trail, and including the memorial grove to British air-crew shot down in World War 2.

Resume your journey through Middelfart, at the end of which you bear right on the road to Udby (No. 313). The route is pleasantly rural with Common Market-inspired large fields growing cereal crops. If you are interested in antiques and bygones divert left to Gelsted and to Hønnerup and visit Hønnerup Hovgård, returning to the 313.

Go through Assens and then at Hårby (on road 323) follow the signs to Fåborg. You will pass through the little village of Faldsled, and see on the right the Faldsled Kro which is renowned for its cuisine (but is expensive). A little further on look for the sign on the left to *Steensgaard Herregårdspension*. A former manor house and now an hotel, it is out of sight of the road at the end of a long tree-lined drive. It dates back to 1535, although the main building is 17th century, and it lies in 27 secluded acres of parkland beside a small lake.

In spite of its substantial bulk, there are only 15 bedrooms, while there are several elegant sitting rooms in different styles of decoration. Dinner is served in the candle-lit red and gold dining room. You can walk in the grounds, play tennis or ride (stables only a few yards from the house).

Apart from the delightful atmosphere of Steensgaard, it also makes an admirable base from which to explore the south of Funen. Less than five miles away is *Fåborg*, a pleasant little town which is best explored on foot (the main street is pedestrianised). See the Vesterport, one of the few remaining town gates in Denmark; the museum of cultural history in the old merchant's house (Den Gamle Gaard); and the Fåborg Museum. Just outside the town is Kaleko Mølle, an old water mill and now a museum, while at nearby Horne is the only round church on Funen.

If you take road 8 towards Kværndrup look for the sign on the left to Egeskov (**58**), Denmark's finest renaissance castle. The castle is now open to the public in summer and you can stroll round the spacious grounds and gardens and there is also an interesting vintage transport and carriage museum. On the way, just beyond Korinth, there is Brahetrolleborg, a substantial manor house.

Odense (**56**) the birthplace of Hans Christian Andersen, should also be visited and there is enough there to occupy a full day without any problem. The quickest way is on road 8 to Kværndrup and then left on road 9. Definitely not to be missed is an excursion to *Svendborg* (**59**), a pleasant town which has a lovely location on the Sound.

One day should be earmarked for a trip to the island of *Ærø* (**61**). You can take the ferry from Fåborg to Søby or from Svendborg to Ærøskøbing (or go from one and return to the other). This is a really beautiful little island, while Ærøskøbing is quite idyllic. Marstal, the island's other town, may not be quite as

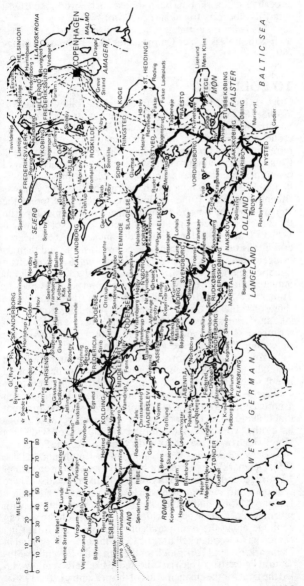

appealing as Ærøskøbing but it should not be overlooked. On a sunny day the ferry trip alone is well worthwhile.

There are other things to see and places to go in this area: such as the little island of Thurø and the bigger island of Tåsinge (**60**).

TO LOLLAND

Drive via Fåborg to Svendborg (road 44) and follow the signs to *Tåsinge* (**60**) which is reached by a lengthy bridge across the Sound. Shortly afterwards turn left to Troense, a very picturesque village with its interesting maritime museum. For refreshments try the Hotel Troense which is almost next door. Continue on the minor road to Valdemars Castle which enjoys a beautiful setting and has a museum of interiors and a good restaurant. Keep to this minor road, bearing right so that you pass Bregninge church. If the day is clear, climb to the top of the church tower, the view from which is highly rewarding. Opposite the church is an interesting little cottage museum. Not far away at Vornæs is an unusual mechanical doll museum. At the nearby crossroads turn left and continue across Tåsinge, and then by bridge and causeway to the island of *Langeland* (**62**). Bear left on the Spodsbjerg and Lohals road. Keep to the Lohals road at Simmerbølle and enjoy the rolling rural countryside to Tranekær. At the end of this village, on the right, is the impressive shape of Tranekær Castle. You can walk round the grounds and lake and if you are seeking food and drink there is a cafeteria in the former stables or you can go back into the village and visit the welcoming Tranekær Gjæstgivergaard inn.

You can either return on the same road to Simmerbølle and then take the Spodsbjerg road or work your way back along a minor road through Stengade. At Spodsbjerg there is the ferry connection (45 minutes) to Tårs, on Lolland. Having driven ashore, continue on road 9 to Maribo. It will soon be apparent that Lolland is flat, but don't let that put you off because it does have other virtues. In the centre of *Maribo* is the Hvide Hus Hotel which overlooks a park and a sizeable lake, the Søndersø.

Between Maribo and Bandholm is Knuthenborg Park (**75**), Denmark's largest manor house park covering an area of 1,500 acres and enclosed by a granite wall, five miles long. There is also a safari park through which you can drive for 10 miles. Linking Maribo and Bandholm is a preserved railway with several vintage steam engines (**76**) ☆. From Bandholm you can continue along the road paralleling the coast. At Birket the church has a wooden bell tower *c*.1350, the oldest of its kind in Denmark. Beyond Torrig look for the sign to the Reventlow Museum at Pederstrup which is dedicated to Count Reventlow who led the fight for the emancipation of the peasantry in the 1780's.

In the opposite corner of the island at *Nysted* is Ålholm Castle (**77**), the history of which dates back to the 12th century. One wing is open to the public and this is *c.*1500 but was rebuilt in 1889. Nearby, on part of the castle estate, is the Ålholm Motor Museum ☆ which has a very fine collection of old motor vehicles. From here a replica of an 1850's steam train runs to the coast. The little town of Nysted is rather quaint, with narrow streets and old houses.

TO ZEALAND

Your route from Maribo is along the secondary road to Nysted, so you can include a visit to Ålhom Castle and motor museum on the way. From Nysted follow the signs to Nykøbing on the island of *Falster* which lies neatly between Lolland and Zealand. Take the road (E64) to Gedser and on the outskirts of the town turn left on the road to Sønder Kirkeby and just beyond the village keep to the left to *Stubbekøbing*. The latter claims to be Falster's oldest town and seems to be a quiet little place. It has an interesting motor cycle and radio museum (**73**). A climb up the church tower provides some excellent views towards the islands of Møn and Bogø.

There is a new section of the E4/E64 motorway open together with an impressive pair of bridges which now link Falster and Zealand via the little island of Farø. However you take the road through Nørre Alslev and turn right following the route of the old E4 (now road 153) across the Storstrøm bridge, skirting Vordingborg and take a minor right turn via the 265 where you have to turn left.

Look out for *Mogenstrup* and on the right side of the road you will see the Mogenstrup Kro. This inn is set back from the road and surrounded by trees and the original building is now completely overshadowed by new extensions. There is a splendid restaurant at the rear, overlooking the gardens. There are lounges, several other dining areas and an indoor pool. Altogether an impressive place to stay, offering a friendly welcome while the cuisine is of a high standard.

Within easy driving distance of Mogenstrup are several manor houses, castles and museums whilst there is another island you can visit. Less than four miles from Næstved (a commercial centre and garrison town of no great appeal) is Gavnø Manor (**71**), which is actually on a small island. This three-winged rococo building was built in 1755-58 and possesses Denmark's largest privately-owned art collection. The manor house has a beautiful setting in 34 acres of parkland.

North of Mogenstrup, near Haslev, is Gisselfeld Castle (**72**) which, like so many other Danish castles and manors, has a splendid location. In this case it is in a 100-acre park laid out in the 1870's by an Englishman, H. E. Milner. It was here that Hans

Christian Andersen found his inspiration for 'The Ugly Duckling'. Quite near is another manor house, Bregentved, on Zealand's largest estate.

Between Mogenstrup and Gisselfeld is Sparresholm (**71**), a 17th century manor house, in the farm buildings of which is a large collection of horse-drawn vehicles of all kinds. Closer to Næstved is the famous Holmegård Glassworks (**71**) at Fensmark, where you can see demonstrations of glass-blowing.

One day can be earmarked for a visit to the island of *Møn* (**74**). Take the 265 road to the quiet little town of Præstø where there are two interesting museums: the Doll Museum 'Den lille By' and the fire engine museum.

Now drive south to Kalvehave where the Queen Alexandrine bridge gets you across to the island of Møn. Drive through Stege and on to Borre where you keep left and follow the signs to Liselund. Within the beautiful park is a romantic little chateau, often referred to as the Danish 'Petit Trianon'. Also within the park are three 18th century summerhouses, the 'Chinese House', the 'Norwegian House' and the 'Swiss Cottage'. Beyond the park and below the cliffs is the sea. Altogether a very pleasant place to pass an hour or two.

From Liselund you can drive a little further south to Møns Klint where five miles of impressive chalk cliffs rise up over 400 ft from the Baltic. A short diversion is to drive down the minor road to Klintholm Havn where there are two good fish restaurants and also an attractive self-catering holiday centre. If you are seeking a longer excursion then it is only about 50 miles to Copenhagen so a day trip is quite easy.

TO JUTLAND

From Mogenstrup take the ring road around Næstved and then road 22 to Slagelse where you join the E66 to Halsskov. This is the ferry port for crossing the Great Belt to Knudshoved on Funen (crossing time 50 minutes).

Alternatively you can use the 265 from Næstved, via the little town of Skælskør to Halsskov. This passes another attractive inn, the Menstrup Kro, which I can recommend. From Knudshoved keep on the motorway which now bypasses Odense but then take the 161 to Vissenbjerg and then turn right on the 335 to Morud. Here you turn left and continue through Stillebæk and Harndrup. This takes you through an enjoyable slice of Funen countryside. At the approach to Middelfart you rejoin the E66 just before the Little Belt suspension bridge. Shortly afterwards follow the E67 signs to Vejle.

Keep on the main road into Vejle (avoiding the E3 motorway) and when you come down by the harbour look for the right turn to *Munkebjerg*. This road runs along the south bank of the very attractive Vejle Fjord. After about three miles the road turns inland quite steeply and actually has several hairpin bends before reaching the summit. This is where you will see, on the right, the entrance to the Munkebjerg Hotel. I have extolled the virtues of this hotel on other pages, so I will simply say that it is a very good place to stay: welcoming, comfortable with excellent food and amenities. You can walk in the woods or borrow one of the hotel's bicycles or take a swim in their pool or play tennis. The Vejle golf course is near.

In *Vejle* (**17**) you can take a boat trip on the fjord or make excursions to a number of places of interest: Givskud (**16**) for the safari park or Jelling (**15**) for the burial mounds and runic stones; or to Glud (**18**) for an interesting museum with several reconstructed buildings and many bygones and artefacts. Further afield is Silkeborg (**24**) in the heart of the Danish lake district. Leave Vejle on road 13 to Tørring, then right through Åle to Brædstrup and then left on road 52. At Rodelund turn right so you can go up to Himmelbjerget – the 'heavenly mountain' – and continue through Ry and Laven to Silkeborg. Return on road 52 to Horsens and south to Vejle on the E3.

TO ESBJERG

There only remains your return to Esbjerg. Leave the Munkebjerg in good time and take the secondary road out of Vejle via Ødsted and Egtved to Brørup, crossing the E66. At Foldingbro, join road 32 to *Ribe* (**8**). Spend as long as you can in this charming old town before motoring the final 20 miles to Esbjerg in time to catch your ferry.

Guide mileages:
Esbjerg – Steensgaard 99 miles; Steensgaard – Maribo 75 miles;
Maribo – Mogenstrup 70 miles; Mogenstrup – Vejle 109 miles;
Vejle – Esbjerg (via Ribe) 75 miles.

ACCENT ON ZEALAND

This ITINERARY offers some notable contrasts: large towns and minor villages, beautiful beaches and the capital city, a small island and varied scenery. You begin by motoring north-east through Jutland to Denmark's second largest city, Århus. Two nights give you time to see some of the attractions before returning south to Hov for the ferry to Samsø.

After a quick exploration of this delightful island, another ferry takes you to Zealand where your next base is Holbæk. You should spend at least two nights here although three nights would be better. You would then have time for a more extensive exploration of the surrounding district, including a visit to the cathedral town of Roskilde. Now you head towards north Zealand and Helsingør. Two or three nights will give you the opportunity to visit some of the castles, museums, beaches and lakes that are to be found in this area.

From Helsingør it is a short drive down the coast to Copenhagen where, depending on the time at your disposal, you can stay for two or three nights. Denmark's friendly capital will easily absorb all your time before heading westwards to Halsskov and across the Great Belt by ferry to Knudshoved and an overnight stay at Nyborg.

The north-east corner of Funen is explored before making for Odense. After one or two nights in this, the birthplace of Hans Christian Andersen, you return to Jutland and across the peninsula to Esbjerg.

The minimum number of nights in Denmark is 10 but it would be preferable to allow 12 or even 14 so that you can make the most of your visit.

DAY 1

For about 24 miles from Esbjerg you keep to the main E66 road to Kolding and Odense before turning left, between Holsted and Vejen on to road 417. This is a pleasant secondary road to Vejle, via Bække. At Vejle join the main road north to Horsens where you can, if you wish, steer clear of the E3 motorway and continue on a secondary road (No. 433) through Solbjerg to Århus.

DAY 2

A day in *Århus* (**28**) to see some of the many things it has to offer. (See the chapter on 'Attractions for Children and Adults'). The 'Old Town', the Museum of Prehistory at Moesgård and the cathedral should be high on your list. For details of hotels see the 'Jutland Only' itinerary.

DAY 3

Take the 451 south from Århus and at Odder (which boasts Europe's oldest distillery) follow the signs to Hov, a village with a small harbour and marina. From here you take the ferry to the

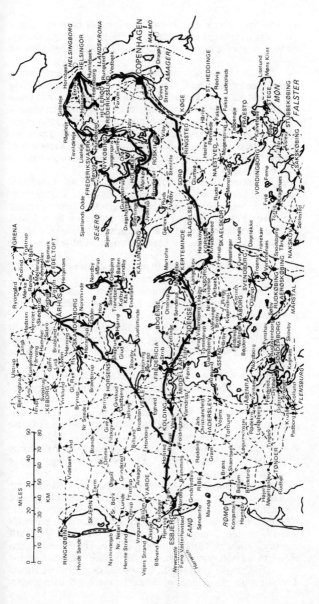

island of Samsø (crossing time 80 minutes; make sure you have a car reservation as capacity is limited). The ferries are quite modest vessels but the crossing makes an enjoyable interlude from driving.

Samsø **(32)** is a pretty little island with its undulating countryside of fields and forests. Having come ashore at Sælvig you should turn left on reaching the main road (the only main road in fact) and drive through Mårup and Nordby. The latter is particularly picturesque and after pausing there continue towards the very tip of the island at Issehoved. The road narrows and then becomes a track and when the track ends that's where you park. From this point you can walk to the cliffs or go down to the beach, which is a mix of shingle and sand.

Returning south beyond Mårup take a left turn to the tiny harbour of Langør, which is in a lagoon. Between it and the sea is a reef, the Besser Rev. Rejoin the main road to Tranebjerg, the principal town on Samsø. The island's museum is to be found here and should be seen. Continue through Brundby, with its post mill, to the charming village and splendid little harbour at Ballen.

Continue south through Brundby once more and take the minor road to Brattingsborg, a large villa or manor built in 1871/1898. The park is open to the public and you can also take the unmade road through the forest to the shingle beach, which is a good place for a picnic.

Follow the signs now to Kolby and then to Kolby Kås where you take the ferry to Kalundborg. (More information on Samsø will be found in the chapter on 'Bornholm and the Smaller Islands').

You should spend a little time at *Kalundborg* which, besides being a commercial centre and harbour, has a well preserved townscape around the imposing church with its five spires like sharpened pencil points. It was built in 1170 and is unique because of its daring construction techniques. Also near the church is the town museum. The area to the south of the town, the Asnæs peninsula, is unfortunately spoiled by a monstrous power station and oil refinery. On the peninsula is the baroque castle of Lerchenborg.

Leave Kalundborg on main road 23 and beyond Viskinge turn left to Holbæk, via Snertinge (road 155). *Holbæk* is one of Zealand's oldest towns and it enjoys a good position on the Holbæk Fjord. There is a particularly interesting museum with many furnished display rooms in a complex of nine 17th/19th century buildings. Good shopping centre. The Strandparken Hotel, in the park on the town's outskirts, makes a good base for your stay. Excellent resturant. Also on the southern outskirts is Tveje Merløse church – the oldest in Denmark with twin towers.

DAY 4

If you have only one free day then it is a question of choosing how you will spend it. There are several options which is why you really need a minimum of two days.

SUGGESTION 1 Drive out on the Nykøbing Sj. road (No. 21) but quite early on take a right turn to Mårsø and Udby and continue through Løserup, Kisserup and Avdebo. This will take you right round the Tuse Næs peninsula. It is a placid, gently rolling landscape, offering lovely views of the water from time to time.

Back on the main road you are almost immediately going past the Lammefjord on your right. There is a dam alongside the road and if you stop (there are lay-bys) you can climb to the top and see that the water level is higher than the land. All the ground to the left has been reclaimed – the most major land reclamation project outside Holland. Just beyond the end of the dam, on the right, is Gundestrup Færgekro – the ferry inn – which is where in pre-reclamation days the ferry crossed the fjord.

You can keep to the main road or alternatively turn right through Nørre Asmindrup which brings you right down by Nykøbing Bay. The minor road keeps to the coast all the way into the town. Nykøbing is unexceptional apart from the Anneberg Collection – a large private collection of antique glass. If you take the road to Rørvig (ferry to Hundested) and turn left, past Rørvig church (painted a distinctive shade of yellow), you will reach a superb stretch of beach with very fine white sand. It shelves gently and is ideal for children.

An alternative way back is to take the secondary road, south of Nykøbing Sj. (No. 225), but first you may wish to deviate to Højby to see its church with its well-preserved frescoes. Drive via Høve and Fåreveile, crossing road 155 at Snertinge and road 23 at Jyderup. You will pass on the left the long drive up to Dragsholm Castle, which is now an hotel and restaurant, although the house and park are open to visitors. The Earl of Bothwell, husband of Mary, Queen of Scots, ended his days here as a prisoner in 1578 (obviously not a paying guest). His body is buried in Fåreveile church.

On the outskirts of Jyderup is a large and very pleasant park complete with woodlands and lake (well-placed camping site nearby). Further south is the Bromølle Kro, Denmark's oldest highway inn. You now take a minor road on your left which brings you through Bennebo and Torbenfeld with its church, manor house and home farm. Continue along this road (No. 231) to Ugerløse and then follow the signs to Tølløse. Before reaching the town turn left to Tjørnede where you turn left again.

These meanderings along minor roads take you through the so-called 'Zealand Alps'. Not all that high, but quite impressively hilly scenery for Denmark. You should emerge on to

117

road 57 at Igelsø, where you turn right for the short drive back to Holbæk.

SUGGESTION 2 Leave Holbæk on the road to Roskilde but don't join the motorway (roads 21/23), instead keep to the old main road (No. 156) and watch for signs on the right to Lejre and Ledreborg Castle. This takes you down an imposing tree-lined avenue, nearly five miles long. Ledreborg (1741/50) enjoys a magnificent setting, the main building standing on the edge of a slope with the grounds reaching in terraces to the bottom of the valley and then rising again. The castle and grounds are open to the public. About two miles beyond the castle is the Lejre Research Institute – an historical and archaeological research centre where Denmark's past has been reconstructed. A walk round the site (about two miles) takes you through an iron age village, a stone age working exhibition, past the sacrificial bog and the cultic dance labyrinth of the bronze age, to other examples from the past: weaving and pottery workshops, farmhouses, a forge and so on. Return by the same route to the main road and follow the signs into *Roskilde* (**68**).

Dominating Roskilde's skyline is the cathedral, for centuries the burial place of Danish kings and queens. They are entombed in amazingly elaborate sarcophagi while the light, high vaulted interior of the building is most impressive. Next in importance at Roskilde is the superb Viking ship museum down at the edge of the fjord. You can see the fully restored Viking ships – all 900 years old – as well as watching work being carried out on others under restoration.

There is also the Roskilde Museum in a former merchant's house and in which there is a fine collection of Hedebo embroidery and folk costumes. More unusual is Brdr. Lützhøfs Eftf., which is a shop restored to its appearance in 1910-20. You can look round and also buy merchandise typical of the period. From Roskilde you return to Holbæk on the main road.

This does not by any means exhaust the attractions of the area. You can visit Lake Tissø – Denmark's fourth largest lake. Or visit the fascinating Tramway Museum at Skjoldenæsholm (**69**) with its 30 trams and length of working tramline – all in the middle of glorious countryside. Nearby is the highest point on Zealand (400 ft above sea level) at Gyldenløveshøj. There's a useful little inn – the Kudskehuset – tucked away off the road, look for the sign. Another excursion is to take the ferry from Holbæk to the delightful holiday island of Orø (30 minutes crossing).

DAY 5

From Holbæk take the secondary road which skirts Bramsnæs Bay until you reach road 53 to Frederikssund. Turn left, and when you reach the village of Skibby, turn right along the minor road to Sønderby. The lake on the left is an important bird sanctuary, and shortly after leaving it you will see on the right Selsø church. A footpath from the car park by the church leads down to Selsø Manor which has a most interesting interior which has hardly altered over the last 200 years.

Continue north through the picturesque village of Skuldelev and rejoin road 53 at Gerlev. Instead of turning right over the bridge to Frederikssund, go straight on through the forest with frequent glimpses of the Roskilde Fjord on your right. You come to *Jægerspris,* a rather long straggling little town at the end of which is Jægerspris Castle. Originally a medieval castle, it was subsequently rebuilt by various Danish monarchs. Part of the castle and the park are open to the public. Close by is the Slotskroen, an attractive inn.

Beyond Jægerspris the road continues to the end of the Horns Herred peninsula at Kulhuse where there is a short (eight minutes) ferry link to Sølager, near Hundested. Return to the road junction south of Jægerspris and cross the bridge to Frederikssund which is an industrial town. Turn left and follow the signs to Frederiksværk, which you ignore as this is also an industrial centre. Follow the signs to Ramløse (road 205).

This road goes round the northern end of the Arresø, Denmark's largest lake and originally part of the Roskilde Fjord. The area is quite heavily forested and very attractive. Before you get to Ramløse turn left on a minor road to Tibirke, Tisvilde and Tisvildeleje. This also takes you through a forested area which continues on the left hand side all the way to Tisvildeleje, which is a pretty little holiday resort. It may well get overrun with visitors in the peak summer months because by the excellent sandy beach is a car park of immense proportions – after all it is not that far from Copenhagen.

On leaving, turn left along the minor road which hugs the coastline. There are very many summerhouses along here all the way through Rågeleje to Gilleleje. Near Rågeleje is a big open stretch of heathland and a good camping site. This part of Zealand is a popular holiday area with the Danes, hence the many summerhouses, some of which are now occupied all the year round.

Gilleleje is also very much a resort even though it has a fishing harbour. Although quite pleasant, it has become rather built-up and the same goes for the next seaside town, Hornbæk. In spite of this 'urbanisation' the coastline remains attractive and the road keeps close to the sea all the way to Helsingør.

DAY 6

Helsingør (**67**) and its surrounding area really deserves more than a two night stay. The town was, for over 400 years (1427-

1857), a rich source of income for the Kingdom of Denmark as all ships passing through the Sound had to pay dues. Guarding this lucrative stretch of water was the impressive bulk of Kronborg Castle which is now the town's number one attraction (see the chapter on 'Attractions for Children and Adults'). Today it is a very busy road and rail ferry port with an intensive service to Helsingborg in Sweden. It only takes 25 minutes for the crossing so a quick visit is no problem.

There are other attractions in and around the town: the Øresund Aquarium, the Town Museum, Saint Olai Cathedral, the Marienlyst Castle, originally a summer palace (1587) and now part of the local museum and the Technical Museum. The latter is in two parts at opposite ends of the town. Helsingør has many old houses and streets and these are gradually being restored.

Hotels: Marienlyst, by the sea on the outskirts of the town and forming a large, if rather incohesive, complex with 213 rooms and 64 holiday apartments. Restaurant, bar and the only casino in Scandinavia where you can actually win money. Vast indoor pool with wave making machine, sauna, health studio and sun deck. Makes a very comfortable centre from which to explore north Zealand. Other hotels: Skandia, Pension Brinkly (at nearby Snekkersten). At Hornbæk there is a large modern resort hotel, the Trouville. Youth hostel at Helsingør.

During your stay you should drive out and visit Fredensborg Palace (**65**) completed in 1722, and the spring and autumn residence of the Danish Royal Family. The beautiful park with its views over Esrum lake is open all year round while the palace is only open in July. Only a few yards from the gates is the Store Kro, a large and very superior inn with period furnishings.

Not far away from Fredensborg is *Hillerød* which has grown up around Frederiksborg Castle (**66**). The country's most magnificent renaissance castle, it was built on three small islands in a lake and therefore enjoys a particularly beautiful setting. The castle now houses the Museum of National History. Plenty of places to eat and drink in the vicinity while the Slotsherrens Kro is actually within the castle complex.

After visiting Hillerød, drive through the Gribskov (forest) which lies on one side of Esrum lake and return to Helsingør via Gurre, passing the ruins of Gurre Castle.

DAY 7

The most enjoyable drive from Helsingør to Copenhagen is along the coast road past a succession of small towns which are strung together all the way to the capital. At Humlebæk make a point of visiting the Louisiana museum of modern art (**64**) which is in a beautiful old park overlooking the Sound. The museum features frequent exhibitions by international artists; and films, music, theatre and literature all form part of Louisiana's remit as a centre for the arts.

DAY 8

Copenhagen offers the visitor a wide choice of things to do and see, and some of the more important appear in the separate chapter on the capital. But even this barely does the city justice. Time will be your limiting factor, so select what appeals to you most and let the rest wait for subsequent visits.

DAY 9

Take the line of least resistance, in other words the E4/E66 motorway, making sure you keep to the latter when they split. If the Vikings have grabbed your imagination then leave the motorway at Slagelse and visit Trelleborg (**70**). This has the remains of a Viking settlement with the circular ramparts still visible and a full-size replica of the old living quarters. There are also traces of the original Viking village.

Only 10 miles further west is Halsskov where you take the Great Belt ferry (crossing time 50 minutes, reservation recommended) to Knudshoved on Funen. Leave the motorway a very short distance after driving ashore and follow the signs to *Nyborg*. Originally a medieval town, it is now an important traffic and commercial centre. The town museum, in a well-preserved half-timbered house, gives a good idea of how a prosperous merchant lived in the period 1600-1637. The town also has Denmark's oldest fortress gate (*c*.1600), while the west wing and Knudstårn (tower) of Nyborg castle are still in existence.

Hotels: Nyborg Strand (large, much extended, resort-style hotel overlooking the Great Belt. Restaurant, bistro. Friendly atmosphere, pleasant bedrooms). Hesselet (a de luxe hotel, backed by woodland and overlooking the sea) and Missionshotellet.

DAY 10

Your immediate destination is Kerteminde, formerly an old fishing town and the harbour for Odense. On one side is Kerteminde Bay and on the other Kerteminde Fjord. It is now very popular in summer, especially the beach to the north of the town. Good fish restaurant by the harbour with another tiny little place, which is excellent, nearly opposite. Continue north up the Hindsholm peninsula which has some very enjoyable scenery, passing one or two pretty villages. The road ends at Korshavn, while there is an unmade road to the final point at Fyns Hoved. The area is quite hilly and even has some cliffs, while the beach is shingle. Jægerhotellet; camping site.

On the way back you can turn left beyond Martofte and take the narrow minor road along the coast. Where it swings inland there is a well-placed camping site. You go through Viby, a pretty village with a beautiful old church. There is a narrow un-made meandering road beyond Måle which brings you back to the road from Korshavn, just north of Kerteminde. When you leave the town turn right and at Ladby take a right turn and look for a sign to the Ladbyskibet (**57**). There, in a field, is a small mound where on entering you will find the remains of a Viking ship in which a viking chief was buried around 1,000 years ago.

Follow the signs to Kertinge and turn left, the road taking you past Ulriksholm Castle (on the right). Originally built for King Christian IV, it is now an hotel and restaurant. The attractive grounds with mature trees sweep down to the waters of the Kertinge Nor. After passing the castle turn left and at the T-junction bear right. This brings you to the Nyborg – Odense road (No.160) where you turn right. You will probably arrive early enough in *Odense* (**56**) to be able to do a little sightseeing: the open-air Funen village, or the railway museum or Hans Christian Andersen's house for example. (See the chapter on 'Attractions for Children and Adults'). For hotels see the 'South Jutland, Funen and a Sprinkling of the Islands' itinerary.

An alternative to staying in Odense is to continue round the Kertinge Nor, after passing Ulriksholm, to Munkebo where there is the attractive Munkebo Kro. It's a comfortable place to stay, with good food, and it is quite a short drive on the 165 into Odense.

DAY 11

A little time for more sightseeing or shopping before driving on the E66 to Esbjerg in time to catch the ferry to England.

Guide mileages:
Esbjerg - Århus 95 miles; Århus - Hov 18¹/₂ miles;
Kalundborg - Holbæk 27 miles; Holbæk - Helsingør 86 miles;
Helsingør - Copenhagen 27 miles; Copenhagen - Nyborg 68 miles;
Nyborg - Odense 56 miles; Odense - Esbjerg 86 miles.

FOR A SHORT STAY

IF YOU HAVE a limited amount of time at your disposal, for example a long weekend, there is much to be said for making Esbjerg your base. You can then enjoy a number of excursions to places of interest in the surrounding area as well as exploring Esbjerg itself. An alternative to taking your own car would be to rent one in Esbjerg and it might be worthwhile checking costs or special out-of-season deals to see which would be the most economic arrangement. Scandinavian Seaways also have a number of short stays based on Esbjerg.

The range of places to visit in the vicinity includes the islands of Fanø and Rømø, the delightful old town of Ribe, the magnificent beaches and the heath and woodland which are to be found throughout the area. For children there is the magnetic attraction of Legoland (not open in winter).

You can, of course, get much further afield on a day trip if you wish, to Vejle or Odense for example. But for many the attraction of a short holiday of this kind is to take it easy and to potter about rather than make concentrated forays to more distant parts. In this itinerary I will give you some ideas on how to occupy your time.

ESBJERG

It might be said that *Esbjerg* (**11**) has been founded on fish and ships. It is Denmark's largest fishing port as well as being an important gateway for Danish exports to Britain, while today it is also involved in the offshore oil industry. Although it is now the country's fourth largest town, in 1868 it had only 30 inhabitants and its brief history does mean that it is rather lacking in old world charm. But it is a good shopping centre with a long pedestrianised main street which literally stretches from one end of the town to the other. There is a fair spread of activities available in the immediate area, such as golf, riding, fishing, rowing, bathing, windsurfing and tennis.

To get some idea of the importance of the fishing industry you should visit the fish auction hall, but you have to be there by 7.00 a.m. to see things happening. Another connection with seafaring and fishing is the interesting Fisheries and Maritime Museum , which was opened in 1968 to mark the centenary of the port. It has a large salt-water aquarium which includes every kind of fish living in the sea around Denmark. The museum features a unique collection of fishing equipment, models and many other exhibits and also has a sealarium.

Other places of interest include the Esbjerg Museum, the Printing Museum (Bogtrykmuseet) which illustrates 500 years of printing and at the same time is a working print shop. The Esbjerg Art Museum, which is housed in a modern building overlooking the harbour, is devoted to Danish post-1915 paintings and sculptures. It also has an attractive restaurant with

123

enjoyable views.

On the outskirts of the town is the Fisherman's Memorial Park, another indication of the town's close links with those who earn their living from the sea. Also in the park are the graves of Allied airmen, German servicemen and European refugees who died in World War 2.

Hotels: Hotel Britannia, just off the main square (Torvet) with well-appointed bedrooms, an excellent restaurant, lounge and bar. Widely used by businessmen and well-managed. Scandic Hotel Olympia, modern and overlooking the harbour. Other hotels: Ansgar Missionshotellet (central, comfortable) and Hotel Bell-Inn. Youth hostel. Several camping sites in the area.

Restaurants now include one or two which are making Esbjerg a more interesting place in which to eat. For evening entertainment there are a few discothèques, some of which match the salty character of the town.

Six miles north, and virtually a suburb of Esbjerg, is Hjerting which lies on the coastal road along the Ho Bay. It is difficult to realise that before the development of Esbjerg this place had the principal harbour in the area. Facing the sea is the Hotel Hjerting with its restaurant specialising in fish dishes. A little further north, still on the coast, is the Mårbæk Plantage, a designated open space and characteristic of west Jutland scenery.

EXCURSION SUGGESTION 1

Drive out through Hjerting and follow the signs to Kokspang and Billum. At Billum turn left to Oksbøl, but keep to the bypass and follow the signs to *Blåvand* (road 431). The latter includes many holiday summerhouses and you should continue right to the end of the road near the Blåvands Huk lighthouse. Here you will find a vast beach with sandhills. In the village is the recently modernised Blåvand Kro which has an inviting restaurant.

To the north of Blåvand is a considerable area used by the Danish army for training purposes. This can, at times, be noisy and when driving you should also watch out for large military vehicles. Return along the same road, but enter Oksbøl, and turn left just before the railway crossing. Continue along the minor road parallel with the railway and then bear left to Kærgård where you turn right. For another good beach turn left to Henne Strand, otherwise turn right and then left through the Blåberg Plantage. Here there is a 210 ft high migrating dune which was shaped by sandstorms in the 16th and 17th centuries.

If you continue on the minor road you reach a T-junction where you turn right to Nørre Nebel and Varde (**12**). The latter town is a junction of numerous roads and has, in the Arnbjerg-anlægget (park), a mini-town which shows what Varde looked like in the 1830's. There is also the Varde Sommerland ☆ in the

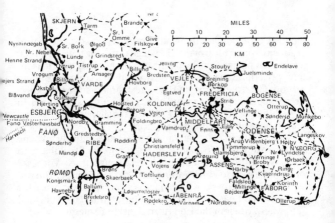

Engpark, an amusement and activity centre for children. From Varde take road 12 back to Esbjerg. If you want to extend this excursion a little, you can turn left, instead of right to Nørre Nebel, and continue to Nymindegab. Here you can take the minor road on the right to Tipperne, on the Ringkøbing Fjord, which is one of Denmark's leading bird sanctuaries (only open on Sundays).

EXCURSION SUGGESTION 2

It isn't essential to have children with you when you visit *Legoland* (**14**) ☆ as there is plenty to fascinate adults. If on the other hand you have children, then a visit will rate the highest priority. Drive out of town on the E66 and a few miles out take the left fork on road 30 to Grindsted. You bypass the town and follow the signs to Billund, where you can't miss Legoland (it's next door to the airport).

Inside this, the largest tourist attraction in Denmark outside Copenhagen, there is a host of things to see. First of all there is the vast Miniland with its imaginative landscapes, towns and villages: Copenhagen harbour, a Norwegian village, part of Amsterdam, the Rhineland, a historic British town and many others involving millions of Lego bricks.

A wild west town, Legoredo, occupies another area, while there are numerous rides: Legocopters, Miniboats, Lego safari cars, the mine train, a timber ride and the giant caterpillar. There is the Traffic School at which children drive miniature cars but have to stick to the rules of the road (and get a driving licence after a successful 20-minute session). Fabuland is for younger children, while other outdoor pleasures include pony rides, panning for 'gold' and baking bread by an Indian wigwam.

Indoors there are more attractions: dolls, old toys and the fabulous Titania's Palace while there is an outdoor puppet show

125

and the Legoland Guards' band. You get a good overall view of Legoland from the top of the 118 ft high revolving tower. You can get an even higher view by taking one of the short, and reasonably priced, excursion flights from the adjoining Billund Airport. Catering is provided by six restaurants and a large cafeteria, while linked to Legoland is the modern Vis-a-vis Hotel. In 1990 Billund will get a new attraction in the shape of a motor and aircraft museum adjoining the airport.

Return to Esbjerg the same way, or alternatively take the Egtved road (No. 176) and then bear right via Skjoldbjerg to Vorbasse, with Randbøl heath away to your left. At Vorbasse look for the road to Hovborg and turn left in the village. You will see the inviting Hovborg Kro which is a good place to pause for refreshments. Leave the village and turn left to Holsted (road 425) where you join the E66 (turn right) to Esbjerg.

EXCURSION SUGGESTION 3

Leave Esbjerg on road 24 to *Ribe* (**8**) and watch for signs into the town. In the centre is the impressive five-aisled cathedral. A climb up the tower is tiring but offers rewarding views. Ribe's preserved townscape is really splendid with its little streets, courtyards and lovely old houses.

Ribe is well endowed with museums: the Bishop's Residence – Hans Tausen's House – is now an archeological museum and the art museum has works by artists from Denmark's 'golden age' of painting. To me the most fascinating museum is Quedens Gård, a four-winged half-timbered merchant's house *c*.1580 which illustrates the long and eventful history of the town.

Saunter along the little quay, Skibbroen and call in at the old Sælhunden inn for refreshments, but first of all have a look at the flood column. By the cathedral is the inviting Hotel Dagmar with its 16th century atmosphere and modern comforts. The elegant restaurant offers good food. On the other side of the cathedral is Weis' Stue, one of Denmark's oldest and smallest inns, *c*.1600.

You can go for a sail on the pleasure boat 'Riberhus' in summer or for something more unusual take the tractor bus to the small island of *Mandø* (**9**) where the 'road' is only negotiable at low tide (don't try and drive there yourself). Mandø has about 100 inhabitants, an inn and a little museum.

After you have exhausted the delights of Ribe, continue south to the island of *Rømø* (**7**) – 10½ miles long, three miles wide and reached along a six mile causeway. It is a mix of moorland, sand dunes and woodland. Good beaches on the west coast.

If you want to return via an alternative route, turn right at Brøns and drive to Gram (where there is a castle, part of which contains a natural history and geology museum). Continue north through Rødding on the 449 to Foldingbro (nice inn) and then follow the signs to Brørup. At the E66 turn left to Esbjerg.

EXCURSION SUGGESTION 4

Opposite Esbjerg, and noticeable when you arrive on the ship from Britain, is the island of *Fanø*. You get to it by one of the busy little ferries from Esbjerg harbour (20-minute crossing). The size of the ferries effectively limits the volume of cars that can invade the island. In summer you can wait hours to get across with your car (in either direction) as there are no advance reservations. So don't plan a tight schedule if you take your car. An intriguing touch is that you can only buy return tickets to Fanø.

The ferry arrives at the 'capital' of the island, *Nordby,* which is a small town with narrow streets. On the west coast of Fanø is a magnificent beach with miles of superb sands, backed by the familiar sandhills. In spite of the low-lying nature of the island it does have scenic variations with moorland, heath and forest. At the south end of Fanø is the gem of the island: the little village of *Sønderho* with its distinctive thatched cottages. In the past Sønderho was a much more active place, building sailing ships and having a busy harbour. It is now very quiet, the harbour is silted up and tourists provide the activity.

In the village is one of Denmark's oldest inns, the Sønderho Kro which opened its doors in 1722. The wife of the present owner is a descendant of the original landlord. It has a small number of beautifully decorated bedrooms while the charming beamed restaurant offers superb cuisine.

There are a few holiday hotels on the island including Fanø Krogaard (Nordby), Kellers Hotel and Hotel Kongen af Danmark (all at Fanø Bad) and Hotel Sønderho (Sønderho). There is also the Feriehotel Vesterhavet, a self-catering centre at Vesterhavsbad. Nine camping sites.

A 300-year-old house is the home of Fanø Museum at Nordby which depicts the life of a seafarer in bygone days. There is also the Fanø Maritime and Costume Exhibition in the Skipper's House (Skipperhuset) at Nordby which features ship models and costumes, while Hanne's Hus, at Sønderho, is the best preserved example of a typical Fanø house. The Sønderho seaman's church, which was built in 1782, includes some beautiful ship models.

Guide mileages:
Esbjerg - Rømø 40 miles; Esbjerg - Ribe 20 miles;
Esbjerg - Billund 36 miles; Esbjerg - Blåvand 24 miles.

LIGHTNING TOUR OF DENMARK

A BRIEF, CURSORY visit doesn't do justice to any country, but there are occasions when time is limited and you have to compromise. If you have only a few days and want to make a fleeting tour of Denmark, then this is the itinerary for you. Although you cover a lot of ground there are plenty of opportunities to stop and see things of interest – more than you might imagine.

You start by taking a roundabout route to Silkeborg, in the heart of the lake district and this will give you a good impression of central Jutland. After an overnight stop you head for Århus, the country's second largest city, and on to Ebeltoft, a pretty little town on the Djursland peninsula.

The following day takes you by ferry from Ebeltoft to Sj. Odde on Zealand. Your eventual destination is Copenhagen, but en route you can take time off to see Roskilde. There are two nights in the Danish capital giving you a chance to see some of the principal attractions before you need to head westwards across Zealand and over the Great Belt to Funen.

Your final night is spent at Odense, the birthplace of Hans Christian Andersen. On the last day you have an easy journey along main roads to Esbjerg. Five nights in Denmark plus one night each way on the ferry means, for example, that you can make this trip from Saturday to Saturday.

DAY 1

Leave Esbjerg on the main E66 to Kolding and Odense and after passing Holsted watch for the crossroads about five miles further east and turn left on to the 417. This secondary road traverses pleasant, if unspectacular, countryside. At Østed turn left to Bredsten and Give (road 441), but at Balle, shortly after crossing road 28, turn right on a minor road past Fårup lake (on the left) to Jelling (**15**). You should pause here to see the burial mounds, the runic stones and the church before joining road 18 to Vejle (**17**).

Vejle provides another opportunity for a brief stop before leaving the town on road 13 (marked to Viborg). You stay on road 13 until Nørre Snede where you turn right (road 453) to Bryrup. Continue to Rodelund where you turn right to Ry (road 445) and along this road look for the sign to Himmelbjerget (on the left). You should have plenty of time to drive up this road, park the car, and walk up by the tower for a magnificent view over the lakes and surrounding scenery.

At Ry, cross the railway, turn left and then left again to Laven. This is a most enjoyable stretch of road with delightful glimpses of the lakes and distant hills. It continues almost all the way to *Silkeborg* (**24**), your first overnight stop. (For details of hotels see 'Mainly Central Jutland' itinerary). In the morning there is time for a quick look round the town and perhaps a visit

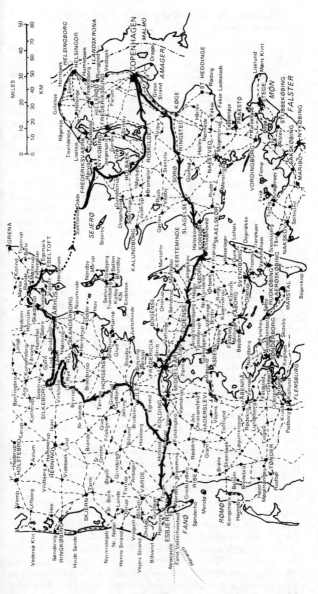

to the Silkeborg Museum to inspect the 2,200-year-old head of the Tollund Man.

DAY 2

Århus (**28**) is your immediate destination and you drive straight there on road 15. A few miles from the city look, on the left, for the Årslev Kro near Brabrand which has a good reputation for its food. When you reach Århus, cross the ring road and continue down Silkeborgvej and watch for the signs on the left to Den Gamle By (the Old Town). As you really only have time to visit one place in Århus, I would recommend that you choose the fascinating Old Town. Return to the ring road, turning right on road 15 signed to Grenå.

At Rønde turn right to *Ebeltoft*. This is a very pleasant route, taking you past the ruins of Kalø castle (on the right) and through Femmøller to Ebeltoft (**34**), your second night stop. (See 'Jutland Only' itinerary for details of hotels). Take a stroll round this picturesque little town on the bay in the evening.

DAY 3

You should be able to squeeze in a quick visit to the preserved wooden frigate 'Jylland' before driving the short distance to the ferry terminal. The Mols Line ferry takes 90 minutes for the crossing to Sj. Odde on Zealand (a reservation is recommended, particularly in summer or at weekends). On Zealand the road runs along the narrow peninsula to Nykøbing Sj. where it swings south-east, past the end of the Lammefjord.

Join road 21 (turn left) at Herrestrup, bypass Holbæk and continue on the 21/23. Turn off to Roskilde, being careful to follow the signs as the junction is a little complex. Roskilde (**68**) has an inner ring road and numerous one-way streets in the centre and several pedestrian-only thoroughfares. The best thing is to head in the general direction of the twin spires of the cathedral and watch out for one of the car parks.

The magnificent cathedral has for centuries been the burial place of Danish kings and queens and gives a good impression of both Danish architecture and history over the last 800 years. From the town centre drive down to the end of the Roskilde Fjord, along Sankt Clara Vej where you will see the Viking Ship Museum. This is a fascinating museum in which are displayed the Viking ships that were recovered from the nearby fjord. Rejoin the motorway and follow the signs to *Copenhagen*.

Two nights are allowed for the Danish capital and what you see during your 'free' day depends very much on your personal taste. More extensive details will be found in a separate chapter, but even this only touches on some of the attractions of the city.

DAY 4

In the morning you could take a sightseeing coach tour which would cover the more interesting places and relieve you of the necessity of driving and parking in the city centre. A stroll down the pedestrian street Strøget is recommended, followed, perhaps, by a trip round the canals and harbour on one of the tourist launches.

You could always drive along the coast road to *Helsingør* and visit the impressive Kronborg Castle. Afterwards you might like to catch one of the frequent ferries to Helsingborg in Sweden (leaving your car behind). The crossing takes only 25 minutes so it is rather fun to go to Sweden for an hour or two. You can make the same sort of trip from Copenhagen to Malmö using one of the hydrofoils.

DAY 5

Your exit from Copenhagen is the E66 (which to begin with is combined with the E4, so make sure you follow the signs when they split). You motor west across Zealand to the Great Belt ferry terminal at Halsskov, crossing over to Knudshoved on Funen (crossing time 50 minutes, make sure you have a reservation to avoid delay). Continue on the motorway until you see the signed exit to Odense (otherwise you will completely by-pass the town).

Odense (**56**) is your last night stop and if you arrive early enough you should be able to do a little sightseeing: a visit to the open air Funen village, or to Hans Christian Andersen's house or the railway museum. For hotels in Odense see 'South Jutland, Funen and a Sprinkling of the Islands' itinerary.

DAY 6

There will be time for some additional sightseeing or shopping before you need to leave for Esbjerg. Rejoin the E66 and after crossing the splendid Little Belt suspension bridge continue westwards across Jutland to Esbjerg. You will have seen a fair slice of Denmark without too much of a rush and hopefully it will encourage you to return for a more leisurely visit.

Guide mileages:
Esbjerg – Silkeborg 95 miles; Silkeborg – Ebeltoft 50 miles;
Ebeltoft – Copenhagen 53 miles; Copenhagen – Odense 88 miles;
Odense – Esbjerg 86 miles.

COPENHAGEN

As THE MAIN purpose of this book is to take you around Denmark I have quite deliberately decided to devote only a modest amount of space to Copenhagen. The Danish capital is well covered in several excellent brochures issued by the Danish Tourist Board as well as in other guides which concentrate on the city.

Copenhagen has several major virtues which make it appealing: it is built to human scale and has been spared the ravages of undisciplined redevelopment; it is easy to get around and you can cover the major part of it on foot; it is visually very attractive; and it enjoys a splendid setting by the sea. To these advantages you can add its excellent amenities and many places of interest. It is a city in which you will very quickly feel at home.

The central focal point is the Town Hall with its 346 ft high tower and in front of which is the broad sweep of the Town Hall Square. To one side, only a few yards away, is the boundary of Denmark's biggest single attraction: Tivoli Gardens. Opened in 1843 and spread over 20 acres in the city centre, it is a marvellous mix of gardens, fountains, restaurants, fun fair, theatre, side-shows, pantomime, band stands and much more. It enjoys a completely unique atmosphere that appeals to both young and old. Everyone goes to Tivoli.

On the opposite side of the Town Hall Square is the start of Strøget, the series of pedestrian shopping streets which stretch all the way to Kongens Nytorv. Here you will find the Royal Theatre, home of the Danish national ballet as well as opera and drama. Close by is the end of Nyhavn, the stretch of water leading to the harbour. For many years it had a slightly doubtful reputation with its succession of seedy bars but now it is largely occupied by new restaurants (some of which are excellent).

A few minutes' walk from Kongens Nytorv is the Amalienborg Palace. It is not one building, but four, one of which being the home of the Danish Royal Family. When the Queen is in residence you can see the changing of the guard in the morning at 11.30. Continue beyond the palace and you soon reach Churchill Park, the Danish Resistance Museum, St. Albans (the English church) and the magnificent Gefion fountain. Now you are at the beginning of the Langelinie which will bring you within sight of the Little Mermaid, the city's most famous statue. She sits, small and forlorn, on a rock gazing out to sea. Returning to the city centre, go down Bredgade and see the beautiful domed Marmorkirken (Marble church).

To one side of Strøget lies the university quarter with its jumble of small streets with their bookshops, antique dealers, boutiques and pavement and cellar cafés. Also within this district is the Rundetårn – the unusual round tower, 115 ft high. You get to the top up a spiral sloping walkway (no lift, no stairs – and Peter the Great of Russia rode up on his horse followed, no less, by the Empress in a horse-drawn coach).

Museums, including some very fascinating ones, abound in Copenhagen: the City Museum, the Royal Museum of Fine Arts, the Rosenborg Palace (now a museum of the Royal Family), the Glyptotek Museum, the National Museum, Thorvaldsens Museum, the Museum of Decorative Art and, on a lighter note, the Toy Museum and Louis Tussaud's Wax Museum. These are just a few of them. On the city's outskirts is another museum of note: the open air museum at Sorgenfri, with its collection of old buildings from all over Denmark which have been assembled on a 90 acre site. New attractions include the biggest planetarium in northern Europe (opens 1989) and the veteran train ferry Sjælland which is a combined restaurant and museum.

It is the same with churches and public buildings; there are many, and a lot of them are worth looking at for their architectural beauty if nothing else. There is the Stock Exchange with its famous spire of four intertwined dragons' tails and Our Saviour's Church, across the harbour on Christianshavn. It has a staircase spiralling around the outside of the spire, while inside is a vast and highly ornamental organ.

There are the statues, like the fisherwoman near Højbro Plads, or a pensive Hans Christian Andersen in a corner of the Town Hall Square or the Lur Blowers also near the square. (The two at the top are supposed to blow their Lur horns when a virgin passes by, but they have been silent for a long time now.)

The city has some nice gardens and parks, especially the King's Gardens and the Botanical Gardens. Entertainment is varied: circus, theatre, ballet, music (classical, jazz, folk and rock), cinemas, discos, some nightclubs while sex clubs and porno cinemas are still around but much less in evidence than in the past.

On the outskirts in the deer park is Bakken, another amusement centre which is more on the lines of a traditional fun fair. The seaside is right at the city's front door and you can easily go across to Sweden on a hydrofoil (40 minutes to Malmö). You should also take a trip on one of the harbour launches, while a city sightseeing tour by coach will let you see all the principal sights without the effort of driving and parking.

There is a good network of bus and local train services (S-trains) and, if you would prefer to forget the car for a day or two you might find the Copenhagen Card worthwhile. This provides unlimited travel on buses and local trains within the metropolitan region (which, for example, stretches all the way to north Zealand) and free entry to a large number of museums and places of interest; you also go half price on the ships and hydrofoils to Sweden. The cost is D kr 80 for one day, D kr 140 for two days or D kr 180 for three days.

Two free attractions which are worth mentioning are conducted tours of either the Carlsberg or Tuborg breweries.

When it comes to food and drink Copenhagen has a very wide range of restaurants, cafés, bars and pubs to tempt the visitor. There is a useful colour brochure available called Restaurants in Copenhagen (price Dkr 10) which lists and describes over 50 in various price categories. Copenhagen This Week (which you will find in hotels) provides an extensive list of restaurants of all kinds plus entertainment, places of interest, hotels, and what's on. Get hold of a copy when you arrive and study it.

Hotels cover the whole spectrum of accommodation from small, simple establishments to the de luxe category. The latter include the Royal (near Tivoli), Scandinavia (off-centre), D'Angleterre (traditional, Kongens Nytorv) and Sheraton (10 minutes' walk from Town Hall Square).

A few examples of other hotels are: Sophie Amalie, Admiral (by the harbour and Amalienborg Palace), Nyhavn 71 (skilful conversion of an old warehouse), Imperial (central, own car parking), Plaza (by the station and Tivoli), Ladbroke Palace (in Town Hall Square), Richmond and Mercur (both close to the centre) and Opera (near the Royal Theatre). Near the station is Helgolandsgade, Copenhagen's so-called 'sleeping street' because it includes so many hotels. Among those in the medium price bracket are the Hebron, Triton, Selandia and Absalon.

There are also hotels outside the city centre which avoid a parking problem. Among these are the Hellerup Park Hotel, Hotel Eremitage, Gentofte Hotel and the Hotel Marina (nice position, on the coast road at Vedbæk, overlooking the Sound). There are several camping sites within the Greater Copenhagen area and also three youth hostels.

This has been a fleeting description of the Danish capital, but it should give you sufficient information to judge the style and character of this highly enjoyable city.

BORNHOLM

ALTHOUGH IT IS inescapably Danish, Bornholm is an island apart. It lies in the Baltic, 85 miles from the rest of Denmark, but less than 25 miles from Sweden. It has all the geographical features of Denmark and more: for example its rocky coastline, which alternates with dunes and cliffs, is unique. It claims to have the best climate in Denmark and its economy is largely based on tourism.

I have to admit to being enchanted by this island with its relaxed atmosphere, more akin to the Mediterranean than Scandinavia. There is an overnight ferry service from Copenhagen to Rønne, the principal town, which is maintained by two large, modern vessels. Unfortunately your night is short as you dock at 6.30 a.m. But if the weather is good it is worth rising early to enjoy the morning arrival.

The town of *Rønne* is concentrated behind the harbour in an elevated position. It has a busy centre with some nicely preserved buildings. The Bornholm Museum is interesting and extensive and gives you a good idea of the history and background of the island (the maritime section, almost in the roof, shouldn't be missed if you like ship models). The ashlar-built church *c.*1300 has a half-timbered tower. Hotels: Griffen (large, modern, on the outskirts), Missionshotel (by the harbour), Hoffmann, Skovly, Ryttergården (edge of town, modern), Fredensborg (a mile out of town, see description later in this chapter).

Driving north from Rønne there is an extensive wooded area between the road and the coast, giving endless opportunities for walking. In fact, all over the island, there are really splendid places to walk or cycle. Take the secondary road, which cuts through this wooded area, to *Hasle,* a small town with a fishing harbour. It is typical of the island's townships with its steep little streets and jumble of buildings. Hotel Herold (perched above the harbour, homely).

Continue on the Allinge road and after about a mile take the left turn to Helligpeder. You are by the water with only a few yards of rocky foreshore on one side and tree-clad cliffs on the other – a delightful road passing occasional herring smokeries (a constant feature of Bornholm) until it ends at Teglkås.

Return to Helligpeder Odde turning left up a steep little lane which will bring you out on the Allinge road again. Watch for the left turn to Vang and go down another steep lane to this pretty little village with its tiny harbour (on the way down is La Port restaurant on the left).

Back on the Allinge road and once more in a forested area, look for the sign on the left to Hammershus, Denmark's largest castle ruin. It lies on a rocky plateau, overlooking the Baltic and 243 ft above sea level. It forms a remarkable complex of buildings and is worth exploring. This area has an impressive granite landscape interspersed with abundant vegetation.

At *Sandvig*, which stretches round the coast to link up with Allinge to form a twin town, you can go a little further and finally walk to the northernmost point, Hammer Odde. Sandvig deserves to be called picturesque with its steep streets and colourful houses. Watch out for the street which narrows down to only 6 ft 6 in! You have now turned south, through Mellembyerne (literally 'between towns') to *Allinge*.

Both Sandvig and Allinge are holiday resorts with an abundance of hotels, pensions and restaurants. Among the hotels are the Pepita, Strandslot, Strandhotellet, Abildgaard, Friheden and Hammersø.

The cliff-top road south keeps to the rocky coast through Sandkås and Tejn, the latter having a modern fishing harbour. You come to what is arguably the most attractive town on the island, *Gudhjem*. From above, you look down on an untidy pattern of red-tiled rooftops, while narrow little streets descend steeply to the harbour. The rocky coast contrasts with the colourful houses, the white smokeries, the green of the trees and the blue of the sea. Hotels: Casa Blanca (overlooks the town), Jantzens Hotel, Therns Hotel.

From Gudhjem, motor inland to Østerlars to see Bornholm's biggest round church, 59 ft in diameter and dating from the 12th century. Round churches are a feature of the island and they were built both for worship and defence. Return to the coast road, travelling south-east to *Svaneke*.

This is another idyllic little township with its fishing harbour, beautiful surroundings and well-preserved houses. By the harbour, and almost adjoining, are two inviting hotels – Siemens Gaard and Østersøen. You continue this coastal route as you turn south through Årsdale to *Neksø*. This is the island's second biggest town and a major fishing port.

Inland from Neksø is Paradisbakkerne (paradise hills) a splendid rocky area of forest and lakes, rift valleys and National Trust heathland. Keeping to the coast you pass through the holiday resort of Balka (Hotels: Balka Strand and Balka Søbad) and reach *Snogbæk*, another fishing village, with a number of picturesque houses.

You are now in the south-east corner of the island and instead of following the inland route to Rønne, keep to the coast, although the road is separated from the sea by a continuous belt of forest.

Look for the left turn to *Dueodde*. The road goes through the forest, and when it comes to an end, walk over the extensive sandhills to the superb beach with its miles of fine white sand. Among the trees is the Dueodde Badehotel. A noticeable landmark is the lighthouse, 153 ft high, where you can climb the staircase (196 steps) to the balcony at the top. From there the views are sensational and definitely worth the exertion required.

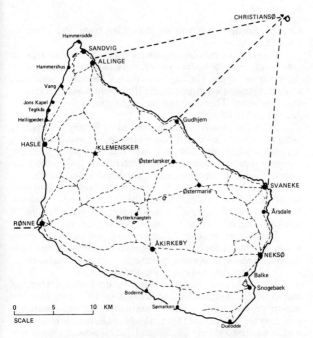

Continuing along the coast road there are numerous turnings leading down to the beach. At Vestre Sømarken you have to turn inland and rejoin the main road but a few miles further west you can again turn left to the little hamlet of Boderne (Hotel Pension Boderne). You are now only a few miles from Rønne, your original starting point; the circumference of the island is about 100 miles.

Inland there are other attractions. Almost in the centre of the island is the extensive Almindingen forest, Denmark's third largest (5,900 acres). It has varied vegetation, ponds and small lakes. At Rytterknægten is the highest point on Bornholm, 530 ft above sea level. A tower affords extensive views over the forest. There are numerous walks including one into the echo valley (Ekkodalen).

As elsewhere on the island, there are plenty of picnic places, ample car parking, refreshment kiosks and toilets. South of the forest is the old market town of *Åkirkeby* which was the island's most important centre in the Middle Ages. It has an unusual stone church *c.* 1150 and some interesting old buildings.

The only other inland centres of any size are Østermarie and Klemensker which are really only large villages. The remaining areas are almost entirely agricultural and provide a pleasant

137

rural backdrop when you are motoring from one place to another.

Between Bornholm and Sweden lie some more Danish possessions – Ertholmene, a cluster of islands 10½ miles from the north-east coast. The biggest island is *Christiansø,* which has some fortifications dating from the 18th century and rich and exotic vegetation. There are regular boat services from Svaneke, Allinge and Gudhjem.

With Bornholm's economy based so largely on tourism there is an abundance of hotels, pensions, summerhouses and restaurants. Camping sites are also plentiful, some of them enjoying superb locations, while youth hostels will be found at Rønne, Dueodde, Svaneke, Gudhjem, Sandvig and Hasle.

The other element in the island's economy is fishing and therefore fish of all kinds feature very largely on restaurant menus. Smoked herring is the major speciality while Bornholm smoked salmon is claimed to be the best in Scandinavia.

I stayed at the Hotel Fredensborg, just outside Rønne, which overlooks the sea. It has modern, well-furnished bedrooms and also self-catering apartments. It has good restaurants, one of which is devoted entirely to fish dishes.

In spite of catering for so many visitors Bornholm has not lost its essential character and personality. Of the visitors, the majority come from Germany, while many are from Sweden. It is probably the only part of Denmark where German is much more widely understood than English and there is a noticeable dearth of literature in English.

An alternative route to the island is via Sweden. From the outskirts of Copenhagen you take the Dragør – Limhamn ferry (50 minutes) and drive to Ystad. From there a ferry runs to Rønne (2½ hours) with two to five sailings a day. New ferry services are due to be launched between Simrishamn (Sweden) and Rønne and Allinge. You can also take a day excursion by hydrofoil from Rønne to Kolobrzeg in Poland.

THE SMALLER ISLANDS

Læsø In the Kattegat. Ferry from Frederikshavn (90 minutes). 2,700 inhabitants, 150 hotel beds, two camping sites, youth hostel. Scenery is a mix of salt meadows, heath, dunes and woodland. A distinctive feature is the use of seaweed for thatching. Two small museums. Bird sanctuary.

Fur Small island in the Limfjord. Interesting geological deposits and moler cliffs. Museum. Inn, camping site. Ferry from Branden (five minutes).

Mors In the western part of the Limfjord with bridge connections to the Thy and Salling areas of Jutland; ferries across the Feggesund (five minutes) and Næssund (five minutes). Principal town Nykøbing M. Attractive Pakhuset Hotel. There is an interesting museum.

Varied scenery with imposing cliffs in the north. At Feggeklit there is a remarkable plateau of moler clay.

Near Sallingsund is the Jesperhus Blomsterpark and numerous camping sites. Youth hostel at Nykøbing M.

Anholt Small island in the Kattegat with 160 inhabitants. Unique sand dune 'desert' landscape. Inn, camping site. Ferry from Grenå (2½ hours). During the Napoleonic Wars the island was occupied by the British and became H.M.S. 'Anholt'.

Hjarnø In the Horsens Fjord. Camping site. Ferry from Snaptun (six minutes).

Endelave Between the east Jutland coast and Samsø. Camping site. Ferry from Snaptun (70 minutes).

Samsø A beautiful island between Jutland and Zealand. 4,875 inhabitants. Ferry from Hov (Jutland) to Sælvig (80 minutes) and from Kalundborg (Zealand) to Kolby Kås (two hours).

See description in the itinerary 'Accent on Zealand'. Varied scenery. Interesting museum at Tranebjerg. In the south is the picturesque little harbour of Ballen; in the north there is the pretty village of Nordby. The tiny harbour at Langør is protected by a long reef.

Hotels: Flinch's (Tranebjerg), Nordby Kro, Pension Verona (Nordby), Ballen (Ballen), Brundby (Brundby), Færgekroen (Kolby Kås). Four camping sites. Youth hostel.

Fanø The island facing Esbjerg from which the ferry sails to Nordby (20 minutes). Superb beach on the west coast. Described in the itinerary 'For a Short Stay'.

Mandø Unusual island in that it is reached from Ribe by a tractor bus at low tide. Inn. Small museum.

Rømø Linked to west Jutland by a long causeway. Varied scenery, good beaches on the west coast. More information in the itinerary 'South Jutland, Funen and a Sprinkling of the Islands'.

Als Quite a substantial island off the south-east coast of Jutland. Linked by bridge to the latter, also ferries to Funen (Fynshav – Bøjden, 50 minutes) and Ærø (Mommark – Søby, 65 minutes). Principal town is Sønderborg which is quite appealing and a good centre. Nordborg, in the north, is dominated by industry. Augustenborg is smaller, and a pleasant little town. Enjoyable countryside.

Årø Reached in seven minutes by ferry from Årøsund on the east coast of Jutland. Camping site.

Bagø Off the west coast of Funen. Ferry from Assens (35 minutes).

Lyø, Bjørnø and Avernakø A trio of small islands reached by ferry from Fåborg on Funen.

Ærø This beautiful island is described in the itineraries 'South Jutland, Funen and a Sprinkling of the Islands' and 'Loitering with Intent'. Three ferry routes: Ærøskøbing – Svendborg (75 minutes), Søby – Fåborg (60 minutes) and Marstal – Rudkøbing (60 minutes).

Strynø A minor island between Ærø and Langeland. Ferry from Rudkøbing (35 minutes).

Tåsinge A delightful island facing Svendborg. Linked by bridges to Funen and Langeland. The little village of Troense is especially charming. See additional details in the itinerary 'South Jutland, Funen and a Sprinkling of the Islands'.

Thurø Horseshoe-shaped island wedged between Funen and Tåsinge. Causeway to Funen, just outside Svendborg.

Orø In the Isefjord and almost surrounded by Zealand. Ferry from Holbæk (30 minutes) or Hammer Bakke (six minutes). 650 inhabitants. Inn, over 1,000 summerhouses. 13th century church, small museum. Scenery unexceptional.

Sejerø Thin slip of an island off the north-west coast of Zealand. Camping site. Ferry from Havnsø (60 minutes).

Agersø and Omø Two adjoining islands at the southern end of the Great Belt. Ferry from Stigsnæs, near Skælskør, on Zealand (Agersø 15 minutes, Omø 40 minutes).

Fejø and Femø A pair of islands off the north coast of Lolland. Ferry from Kragenæs (Fejø 15 minutes, Femø 50 minutes). Camping site and inn on each island.

Bogø Between Falster and Møn. Causeway from Møn linked by bridge on Farø. Ferry to Stubbekøbing, Falster (12 minutes).

HELPFUL GENERAL INFORMATION

Alphabet Don't forget that Danish has 29 letters in its alphabet. After A to Z comes Æ, Ø and Å. Bear it in mind when looking in the telephone directory or any index. (The index in this guide follows the Danish style, just to get you used to it).

Banks Normal hours 9.30 a.m. to 4.00 p.m. (Thursdays 6.00 p.m.). Closed Saturdays, Sundays and public holidays.

British Embassy 40 Kastelvej, DK-2100 Copenhagen Ø. Telephone: (01) 26 46 00.

Chemist In Danish it is an Apotek. It is the only place that medicine can be bought. Many preparations sold without prescription in the UK are only available on a doctor's prescription in Denmark.

Climate Danish weather, like the British variety, is variable. Summer is generally from the end of May to the end of August. It can be enjoyably warm and dry and when it is hot it is seldom humid. As you are never far from the coast there is usually a cooling breeze. Spring and autumn can be very pleasant. Bornholm has the reputation of having the best climate in Denmark.

Currency The unit of currency is the krone (plural kroner). There are 100 øre in a krone. Coins in circulation are: 5 øre, 10 øre and 25 øre and 1 kr, 5 kr and 10 kr. Notes in circulation: 20 kr, 50 kr, 100 kr, 500 kr and 1,000 kr.

Electric current Throughout Denmark it is 220 v AC, 50 cycles. Danish plugs are not the same as those used in Britain so you will need an adaptor.

Emergencies Dial 000 from any public telephone (no charge).

Health service All employees and pensioners from EEC countries and their families staying temporarily in Denmark are covered by Insurance Group 1, which entitles them to free medical care and the refund of a considerable amount of dentists' and pharmacy charges. British citizens who do not fall into the categories above are covered by Insurance Group 2 which entitles them to a more limited refund. Your UK passport or the EEC form E-111D issued by your local authority has to be shown to the doctor or pharmacy. If cash payment is demanded, the refund is paid by the nearest municipal or health insurance office (details from the local tourist office). The refund should be applied for before leaving Denmark.

Although the Danish health service does cover you to a major extent, travel insurance cover is also recommended.

Passports UK visitors to Denmark need to have a standard British passport or a British visitor's passport. A visa is not required.

Post office Normal opening hours 9.00 a.m. or 10.00 a.m. to 5.00 p.m. or 5.30 p.m. Saturday 9.00 a.m. - 12 noon (some offices closed on Saturdays). Closed on Sundays.

HELPFUL GENERAL INFORMATION

Public holidays Maundy Thursday (day before Good Friday), Good Friday, Easter Sunday, Easter Monday; Great Prayer Day (fourth Friday after Good Friday), Ascension Day, Whit Sunday, Whit Monday, Constitution Day (5 June, from noon); Christmas Eve (from noon), Christmas Day, Boxing Day, New Year's Eve (from noon), New Year's Day.

Radio news in English Radio Denmark broadcasts a short news bulletin in English, Monday – Saturday, at 8.15 a.m. on programme III (93.85 MHz).

Telephone Lift receiver and insert two 25 øre coins (local calls) or Dkr 1 coin (long distance calls). Important: your coins are not returned even if the number is engaged, so insert the minimum number of coins. You can repeat your call or make another one if you still have a 'credit'. For assistance in using the telephone dial 00 30. For international calls dial 009 followed by the country code (44 for the UK), then the STD code and finally the subscriber's number. **Note: In 1989 all area codes are being changed – check before dialling.**

Tipping Almost non-existent. Hotel, restaurant and taxi charges include service and you only tip if some special service has been rendered. You don't tip hairdressers, theatre or cinema ushers. About the only exception is leaving 1 or 2 kr for use of the washbasin in staffed ladies' or gentlemen's toilets.

Useful addresses
Danish Tourist Board UK Office: 169/173 Regent Street, London W1R 8PY (entrance in New Burlington Street). Telephone: 01-734 2637.
Danish Tourist Board, H.C. Andersens Boulevard 22, DK-1553 Copenhagen V. Telephone: (01) 11 13 25 for enquiries when in Denmark.
Scandinavian Seaways, Parkeston Quay, Harwich, Essex CO12 4QG. Telephone: (0255) 241234.
DFDS Travel Centre, 15 Hanover Street, London W1R 9HG. Telephone: 01-493 6696.
Scandinavian Seaways, Tyne Commission Quay, North Shields, Tyne and Wear NE29 6EE. Telephone: (091) 2960101.

VAT Called MOMS in Denmark. Current rate is 22 per cent. Normally all prices are quoted inclusive of VAT.

What you can take in Coming from the UK (as an EEC country) you can take into Denmark (by persons over 17 years of age): 1.5 litres of spirits (or 3 litres of strong or sparkling wine). 3 litres of other wine (table wine). 300 cigarettes or 150 cigarillos or 75 cigars or 400 g of smoking tobacco.

As the price of spirits and cigarettes is high in Denmark it is advisable to buy your requirements on the ferry to Denmark.

INDEX

Activity Parks 56, 58, 59, 63, 90, 93, 105, 125
Agersø 140
Agger 31, 90
Aggersund 93
Agger Tange 90
Allinge 136
Almindingen 69, 137
Als 87, 140
Anholt 96, 105, 139
Arresø 119
Assens 104
Augustenborg 140
Auning 63
Avernakø 140

Bagenkop 85
Bagø 140
Bakken 67, 133
Balka 136
Ballen 63, 116, 139
Bandholm 69
Bangsbo Museum 65, 94
Besser Rev 116
Bicycle Museum 63
Billund 58, 81, 98
Bjørnø 140
Blokhus 64, 93
Blåbjerg 89
Blåvand 124
Boderne 137
Bogense 83
Bogø 107, 140
Bornholm 8, 69, 135
Brahetrolleborg 84, 108
Brattingsborg 116
Bregentved 112
Bregninge 66, 85, 110
Brundby 116
Bulbjerg 92
Bønnerup 96
Børglum Monastery 65, 94

Christiansfeld 57, 86
Christiansminde 84
Christiansø 138
Clausholm Castle 63, 105
Copenhagen 8, 67, 130, 132

Dageløkke 31
Danish Tourist Board 142
Danland 31, 90
Dansk Autohjælp 20
Den Gamle By 62, 130
DFDS Seaways 11, 142
Djurs Railway Museum 63, 96
Djurs Sommerland 63, 96, 105
Dragsholm Castle 117
Drejø 85
Dronninglund 95
Dueodde 69, 136
Dybbøl Banke 57

Ebeltoft 63, 96, 97, 105, 130
Egense 95
Egeskov Castle 66, 83, 108
Elsinore - see Helsingør
Endelave 139
Ertholmene 138
Esbjerg 13, 24, 58, 123

Esrum lake 120

Falck 20
Falck Museum 66
Falster 8, 68
Fanø 24, 31, 58
FDM 21
Feggeklit 139
Fejø 140
Femmøller Strand 97, 130
Femø 140
Fjerritslev 64, 93
Flyndersø 62, 103
Foldingbro 98, 113, 126
Fredensborg Palace 67, 120
Frederiksborg Castle 67, 120
Frederikshavn 65, 94
Funen Village 66
Fur 103, 139
Fyns Hoved 121
Fyrkat 64
Fænø Sund 107
Frøbjerg Bavnehøj 86
Fåborg 84, 108
Fårevejle 117
Fårup Sommerland 65, 93

Gammel Estrup Castle 63, 96, 105
Gavnø Manor 68, 111
Gilleleje 119
Gisselfeld Castle 68, 111
Givskud 59, 82, 100, 113
Gjern 62, 102
Gjerrild 96, 105
Glud 59, 82, 113
Gram 126
Great Belt 8, 23, 112, 121, 131
Grenen 65, 94
Grenå 63, 96, 105
Gribskov 120
Grønhøj 93
Gråsten 87
Gudhjem 69, 136
Gurre Castle 120
Gyldenløveshøj 118

Haderslev 57, 86
Hadsund 95
Hals 95
Halsskov 23, 112, 121, 131
Hammer Odde 136
Hammershus 69, 135
Hanklit 64
Hantsholm 92
Hansted Reservat 92
Hasle 135
Havneby 88
Helsingør 67, 119, 131
Henne Strand 124
Herning 59
Hessel 103
Hillerød 67, 120
Himmelbjerget 62, 101, 128
Hindsgaul 86, 107
Hjarnø 82, 139
Hjerl Hede 62, 103
Hjerting 124
Hjørtø 85
Hjørring 94
Hobro 104

Holbæk 116
Holstebro 59, 90
Hornbæk 119
Horne 108
Hornslet 63, 96
Hov 63, 114
Hovborg 99, 126
Humlebæk 67, 120
Hurup 90
Hvalpsund 103
Hvidsten 96

Issehoved 116

Jelling 59, 82, 100, 113
Jesperhus Flower Park 64, 139
Juelsminde 82
Jyderup 117
Jystrup 68
Jægerspris Castle 119

Kaleko Mølle 84
Kalundborg 116
Kalvehave 112
Kalø Castle 97, 106, 130
Katholm 97
Kerteminde 121
Klejtrup Sø 64
Klintholm Havn 112
Klitmøller 92
Knudshoved 23, 112, 121, 131
Knuthenborg Park 69, 110
Kolby 116
Kolby Kås 116, 139
Kolding 58, 86
Korinth 84, 108
Korshavn 122
Krik 90
Kronborg Castle 8, 67, 120, 131
Kulhuse 119
Kværndrup 66, 83

Ladbyskibet - Viking Ship 66, 122
Lammefjord 117, 130
Langeland 8, 67, 85, 110
Langesø 83
Langør 116
Laven 102, 113, 128
Ledreborg Castle 118
Legoland 56, 58, 81, 98, 100, 125
Lejre Research Centre 68, 118
Lerchenborg 116
Lindholm Høje 64
Liselund 69, 112
Lohals 85
Lolland 8, 69
Louisiana 67, 120
Lund Fjord 92
Lyø 140
Læsø 139
Løkken 64, 93
Lønstrup 65, 94
Løvenholm Castle 97

Mandø 58, 126, 139
Marbæk Plantage 124
Mariager 96, 104

INDEX

Maribo 69, 110
Marienlyst Castle 120
Marselisborg Forest 62, 97, 106
Marstal 66, 84, 108
Meet the Danes 71
Meilgård Castle 96, 105
Middelfart 86, 108
Moesgård 97, 114
Mogenstrup 111
Mors 64, 139
Motorcycle and Radio Museum 68, 111
Motor Museums 62, 69, 102, 111
Munkebjerg 82, 98, 100, 112
Møgeltønder 57, 87
Møn 8, 31, 68, 112
Møns Klint 68, 112
Mønsted 62, 102
Mårup 116

Neksø 136
Nibe 64, 93, 103
Nimtofte 96
Nordby (Fanø) 58, 127
Nordby (Samsø) 63, 116, 139
Norsminde 97
Nyborg 121
Nykøbing F 111
Nykøbing M 139
Nykøbing Sj. 117, 130
Nymindegab 89, 125
Nysted 69, 111
Næstved 68, 111
Nørre Vorupør 92

Odder 98, 114
Odense 8, 65, 83, 108, 122, 131
Oksbøl 124
Omø 140
Orø 118, 140

Pederstrup 110
Preserved Railways
  Bryup-Vrads 59, 100
  Helsingør-Gilleleje 68
  Mariager-Handest 63, 96, 104
  Maribo-Bandholm 69, 110
Præstø 112

Randbøl Heath 100, 126
Randers 96
Rebild Hills 63, 95
Reventlow Museum 110
Ribe 58, 88, 98, 113, 126
Rimsø 97
Ringkøbing 59, 90
Ringkøbing Fjord 89, 125
Rodelund 101, 113, 128
Rold Skov 63, 95
Rosenholm Castle 63, 96, 105
Roskilde 68, 118, 130
Roslev 103
Rubjerg Knude 65, 94
Rudbøl 88
Rudkøbing 67, 85

Rugård 97
Ry 101, 113, 128
Rytterknægten 69, 137
Rødby Havn 14
Rømø 31, 57, 88, 126, 139
Rønde 97, 130
Rønne 69, 135
Rørvig 117
Råbjerg Mile 65, 94
Rågeleje 119

Safari Parks 59, 69, 100, 113
Sallingsund 139
Saltum 65
Samsø 63, 116, 139
Sandvig 136
Scandinavian Seaways 11, 142
Sebbersund 93
Sejerø 140
Selsø Manor 119
Silkeborg 59, 102, 113, 128
Sj. Odde 130
Skaføgård 97
Skagen 65, 94
Skanderborg 98
Skarø 85
Skibby 119
Skive 62, 102
Skjoldenæsholm 68, 118
Skørping 95, 104
Snaptun 82, 139
Snogbæk 136
Sommerland West 59, 90
Sorgenfri Open Air Museum 67, 133
Sostrup Castle 105
Sparresholm Carriage Collection 68, 112
Spodsbjerg 110
Spøttrup Castle 62, 103
Steensgård Herregårdspension 85, 108
Stinesminde 95
Store Blåkilde 104
Storebælt - see Great Belt
Storstrøm 111
Struer 90
Strynø 140
Strøget 132
Stubbekøbing 111
Sundsøre 103
Svaneke 69, 136
Svendborg 66, 84, 108
Sælvig 116
Søby 84
Sølager 119
Sønderborg 57, 87, 140
Sønderho 58, 127
Søndersø 110
Søndervig 90

Tambohuse 90
Technical Museum 67, 120
Thingbæk 64, 104
Thurø 84, 110, 140
Thyborøn 90
Tipperne 89, 125
Tissø lake 118
Tisvildeleje 119
Tivoli Gardens 56, 67, 132

Tramway Museum 68, 118
Tranebjerg 116, 139
Tranekær Castle 67, 85, 110
Trelleborg 68, 121
Troense 66, 85, 110
Tønder 57, 87
Tårs 110
Tåsinge 8, 66, 85, 110, 140
Tåstrup 97

Udbyhøj 105
Ulriksholm Castle 122

Valdemars Castle 66, 85, 110
Vang 135
Varde Sommerland 58, 124
Vejle 59, 81, 98, 113, 128
Vestervig 90
Viborg 62, 102
Viking Ship Museum 68, 118, 130
Voldum 63, 96
Vorbasse 100
Vornæs 110
Vrads 100

Ærø 8, 24, 66, 84, 108, 140
Ærøskøbing 24, 66, 84, 108

Øer 97, 106
Østerlars 69, 136

Åbenrå 87
Åkirkeby 137
Ålborg 64, 93, 103
Ålestrup 63
Ålholm Castle 69, 111
Ålholm Automobile Museum 69, 111
Århus 62, 97, 106, 114, 130
Årø 140